Geor

# A Game of Thrones

## BookCaps Study Guide

www.bookcaps.com

# Table of Contents

# Author Biography

George R. R. Martin started his career as a professional writer by writing short science-fiction stories in the early 1970s, several of which went on to be nominated for Hugo and Nebula Awards. When the 1980s came around, Martin started expanding his horizons as a writer, bringing his talents and creativity to the realm of television. In his 10 years of writing and developing pilots and feature films in Hollywood, one of the feedbacks that he most often received were that his scripts, while well-written, often went way beyond what the allocated budget would allow. Consequently, he often had to cut the length and complexity of his scripts to a more manageable level.

In 1991, Martin started working on what would be his critically-acclaimed series, A Song of Ice and Fire. He returned to the series again in 1994 with the intention of writing the best book he could write, one free from the shackles of budgetary constraints that so often showed up during his stint in Hollywood.

And that was how A Song of Ice and Fire begun to take shape. Drawing inspiration from the War of the Roses, the very bloody dynastic struggle that took place in Medieval England in the 1450s to 1480s, Martin weaved history and fantasy elements together, creating a fantasy world that was darker, more violent and felt inevitably more real than any epic fantasy series created so far. 1996 saw A Game of Thrones being published, the first book in Martin's planned series; a following grew around it, surely but surely.

The book went on to win multiple awards and was made into a 10-episode TV series by HBO. The series received critical acclaims for its stellar cast and high production values; such was its popularity that a second season was green-lighted even before the series was midway through. At the time this guide was published, Martin has already completed five books in what he plans to be a seven-book series.

A Game of Thrones is usually classified as fantasy, but many critics and reviews say that it transcends the genre; a lot of the book's fans are people who, before picking up Martin's book, had never even read a single fantasy novel before. It is an excellent book, with many comparing it to JRR Tolkien's Lord of the Ring series, widely acknowledged to have single-handedly given birth to the fantasy genre. High praise for any fantasy book indeed, but it doesn't give Martin proper credit – while there may be some general similarities on the surface, Martin's Westeros is distinctly different from Tolkien's Middle-Earth. If there's a series that comes close to the grandeur of Tolkien's work, it would surely be Martin's A Song of Ice and Fire series.

# Plot Overview

A Game of Thrones differs from most books because the readers see the world through the viewpoints of a huge cast of characters.

The closest thing the story would have in terms of a protagonist and an antagonist would be House Stark and the House Lannister. The Seven Kingdoms of Westeros are under the control of a handful of large and powerful noble houses, known as the Great Houses; House Stark and House Lannister are both Great Houses. Smaller houses pledge fealty to the Great Houses.

The story starts off in Winterfell, the ancestral home of House Stark, called Rulers of the North because they control the North. The body of a direwolf is discovered, its pups still alive and suckling on its teats. This is a bad omen for the Starks, as the Direwolf is the sigil of their House. The Lord of House Stark, Eddard Stark decides not to kill the pups; there are six pups in total, so each of his five children get one, including his bastard, Jon Snow.

Following that, King Robert Baratheon, comes to Winterfell. His entourage includes the Queen, Cersei Lannister, and her brothers, Jaime Lannister and Tyrion Lannister, the latter being a dwarf. The Starks are mystified as to the reasons for the King's visit, but Eddard soon learns it is because King Robert wants to appoint him as the new Hand of the King, a position that would give him no small amount of power because the Hand is more or less the King's right-hand man. Robert reveals that the previous Hand of the King, Jon Arryn, of Great House Arryn, has only recently passed away.

Eddard accepts the King's offer. A feast is held, with many of the northern lords coming to celebrate. Before they set off for King's Landing, Eddard's bastard, Jon Snow, decides to follow his uncle, Benjen Stark, to the Wall, a humongous wall of Ice that stretches across the northern borders of the Seven Kingdoms. The second eldest Stark boy, Bran Stark, well-known for his climbing prowess, mysteriously falls from a tower, and falls into a coma.

On the way to King's Landing, an altercation between King Robert's son, Prince Joffrey Baratheon, and the two Stark girls, Sansa (elder) and Arya (younger) results in Sansa's direwolf being executed, while Arya forces her own direwolf to run away.

When they arrive at King's Landing, Eddard proceeds to dispense justice as the King's Hand. His eldest daughter, Sansa, is betrothed to Robert's Joffrey. After investigating further, Eddard discovers that Jon Arryn was murdered by a very rare, undetectable poison. The reason behind the murder shocks him: it was because Jon Arryn had been poking his nose into the Lannister's affairs, or more specifically into Prince Joffrey's real lineage. His suspicious grown when he is lead to two of King Robert's bastards, a female baby and a young boy who works as an apprentice armorer – both have black hair.

Going further back into the Baratheon history, Eddard discovers that all previous Baratheons were black-haired, even if they married Lannisters, who are famed for their blonde hair. The only exceptions turn out to be Prince Joffrey and his two siblings, Princess Myrcella and Prince Tommen. Eddard arrives at the conclusion that the only reason Robert's children have blonde hair, and not black, are because they are not his –– instead, the three royal children were born from an incestuous affair between the Queen and her brother, Jaime "Kingslayer" Lannister.

Meanwhile, Tyrion follows Jon Snow to the Wall. Jon Snow is disillusioned when he discovers that all sorts of men are recruited to join the Night's Watch; he learns that some of his new brothers are rapists, cowards, thieves and scoundrels. But with some advice from Tyrion and a boy by the name of Sam Tarly, Jon finds contentment at the Wall.

Tyrion then leaves the Wall, stopping by at Winterfell before his ultimate destination of King's Landing. At Winterfell, he offers a gift to Bran Stark, who has since woken from his coma but has forever lost the use of his legs: the plans and designs for a special leather saddle that would allow Bran to ride a horse.

Tyrion then leaves Winterfell and stops at an inn, where he is captured by Lady Catelyn Stark and her retinue of guards. Earlier on, when Bran was still in a coma, a man managed to successful reach his bedroom and tried to kill him; Bran's direwolf foiled the man's plans. Catelyn is surprised at the high-quality of the dead man's dagger and goes to King's Landing to present the dagger to Eddard. She shares her suspicions with her husband: she suspects that the Lannisters were behind the attempt on Bran's life. Eddard then tells her to return to Winterfell to rally the Stark bannermen, and to prepare for war.

Catelyn does so, but by chance, happens to stumble across Tyrion at the inn, and takes him prisoner. With the help of some sellswords, she takes Tyrion to The Vale of Arryn, the ancestral home of Great House Arryn. She seeks to find the truth behind Lysa Arryn's earlier message to her, warning her to stay away from the Lannisters – Lysa is her sister, and also the wife of the late Jon Arryn, the previous Hand of the King.

In the Vale, Lisa Arryn, driven nearly insane by the death of her late husband, agrees to offer Tyrion a fair trial, with her son, Robert Arryn, being the judge. Seeing that Lysa's son would only issue one verdict, one that would end up with him being thrown down the mountain side, Tyrion requests for trial by combat and representation the trial by his brother, Jaime Lannister. Lysa refuses, saying that Jaime is too far away and that the duel would be happening on the same day. Tyrion looks on in despair, but he is saved when Bronn, the sellsword that accompanied Catelyn's party to the Vale, agrees to be his champion.

In the ensuing trial by combat, Bronn defeats Lysa's champion. Lysa releases Tyrion unwillingly, and Tyrion and Bronn head towards the Lannister's ancestral stronghold, Casterly Rock. Along the way, they are ambushed by a pack of savage mountain clansmen. Tyrion convinces them not to kill him by offering to reward them with Lannister steel weapons and armor; they agree and follow Tyrion out of the Vale.

In King's Landing, Jaime Lannister, on hearing of his brother's capture, loses his cool and flees the city, but not before killing several of Eddard's men. Eddard breaks his leg in the encounter with Jaime; when he recovers, Robert makes him King again. King Robert then goes hunting while Eddard tries to do his duties as best as he can.

Shortly thereafter, the King returns from the hunt, grievously wounded after being gored by a boar. On his friend's death bed, Eddard cannot find it in his heart to tell Robert the secret that he's uncovered, that Prince Joffrey, Prince Tommen and Princess Myrcella are not Robert's children, but Jaime's. However, before his death, Robert proclaims Lord Eddard as Lord Regent and Protector of the Realm until Prince Joffrey comes of age.

Eddard then confronts Cersei, revealing the secret of her three children being Jaime's instead of Robert's and offers her the chance to flee King's Landing with the three royal children. He then makes arrangements to convince the 2000-strong City Watch to arrest the Queen and her children if they decide not leave King's Landing.

The Queen, with the aid of her advisors, has her own plans up her sleeves, however, and bribes the City Watch to switch to her side, and they do, taking Eddard by surprise. They take him captive, put him behind bars and declare him a traitor. The City Watch then proceeds to kill every member of Eddard's household that followed him to King's Landing. Sansa is held in her room, but Arya manages to escape, and goes hiding the city's slum area.

When news of his father's capture reaches Winterfell, the eldest Stark boy, Robb Stark, calls the Starks' bannermen. At first, some of the Northern lords cast doubts on Robb's ability to lead, considering his youth. But through his skilled leadership, he soon commands their loyalty. When faced with a two-pronged Lannister attack, one led by Tywin Lannister (the father of Cersei, Jaime and Tyrion) and the other led by Jaime, Robb sends a small decoy force against Tywin's army and wins a resounding victory against Jaime's army, capturing Jaime Lannister in the process.

Meanwhile, on the Wall, Jon Snow is now an official brother of the Night's Watch, and personal steward to the Commander of the Night's Watch himself. He distinguishes himself in duty by protecting the Commander in a battle against a deadly wight, using fire to destroy the undead creature; the Commander rewards him with a sword made from Valyrian steel. However, upon hearing the news of his father's capture, Jon decides to ride off to join Robb's army, but is stopped by his fellow Knight Watch brothers.

Upon his return to the Wall, Jon Snow makes a promise to the Commander that he will no longer run. The Commander then proceeds to lead a sizeable party of Night Watch brothers, including Jon, north of the Wall, with a mission of finding Benjen Stark, who never returned to the Wall after a ranging that took place several months ago.

Back in King's Landing, Lord Eddard does as he is told, in order to save Sansa's life. In front of the public and the King, he pleads guilty to charges of treason; in doing so, he intends to protect Sansa from the Queen and her advisors. He has also been advised beforehand that the Queen would allow him to join the Night's Watch if he pleads guilty. However, Prince Joffrey, totally unaware of the dire consequences of doing so, orders Eddard to be executed. Sansa is nearly driven mad at the sight of her father's execution. Arya bumps into Yoren, a man of the Night's watch, during the execution; Yoren, who considers himself a brother to Eddard Stark due to Benjen Stark being in the Night's Watch, smuggles Arya away from the city.

Upon hearing the news of his Father's death, Robb Stark vows vengeance upon House Lannister. The Northern Lords proclaim Robb Stark as King of the North.

*     *     *

Meanwhile, as all this is happening in Westeros, there stirs other events across the sea, on the eastern continent of Essos.

The Great House Targaryen once ruled the Seven Kingdoms. However, King Robert rebelled against the Targaryen's cruel reign. The last two Targaryens, Viserys and Daenerys, elder brother and younger sister, fled to the east when they were small, and ended doing most of their growing up in the Free Cities. Upon Daenerys' 12th birthday, Viserys offers her as a bridge to the great Khal Drogo, a Dothraki chieftain who has never lost a battle – he offers his sister in exchange for an army, one that he hopes will help him overthrow King Robert's rules and once again return Westeros to the Targaryens. Before the wedding, Viserys and Daenerys meet an exiled knight from Westeros by the name of Ser Jorah Mormont.

At her wedding, the most expensive gifts she receives are 3 dragon eggs, long since fossilized. The eggs are said to be very valuable; each egg can pay for a sizeable army.

The marriage between Daenerys and Khal Drogo is awkward at first, but she soon learns to love him and starts enjoying Dothraki life. She eventually gets pregnant. Her brother, Viserys, is eventually killed by Khal Drogo because of his arrogant manner, threatening Daenerys, and his blatant disregard for the sacred customs of the Dothraki.

An assassin from the Seven Kingdom tries to assassinate Daenerys but fails. Enraged by this attempt at his wife's life, Khal Drogo makes a proclamation in front of the entire tribe: he will take the entire tribe, all 40,000 warriors, to the Seven Kingdom on ships, to tear down the castles of the Seven Kingdoms, and to do it so that his son can sit on the Iron Throne.

However, in a battle with the Lamb People, Khal Drogo suffers a battle injury that eventually kills him; almost all of the warriors then depart, for in Dothraki society, women cannot lead a tribe. Grieving for her loss, Daenerys prepares a funeral pyre, placing the 3 fossilized dragon eggs next to Drogo's body. She then sets the pyre on fire, and proceeds to walk calmly into the blistering inferno. The next morning, Ser Jorah Mormont discovers Daenerys, alive and well, now with three magnificent baby dragons under her control. In awe, Mormont and all the other remaining Dothraki drop to their knees to swear fealty to Daenerys.

And so the story ends.

# Themes

# Honor

In A Game of Thrones, many characters appear to be men and women of honor, at least on the surface. For some, it is no different than putting on a ring or necklace; you put it on when you want to look your best, but take it off when you need to get down to practical matters. For others, honor only becomes a burden when they forced to make a choice.

In the story, there is a chapter where a wise old man tells Jon Snow, a young boy who has just joined the order of the Night's Watch, that it is easy to choose the honorable path when there is nothing at stake; however, when the choice is between love and honor, how many still stay put on the path of honor?

A lot of the characters in A Game of Thrones find the concept of honor impractical and detrimental to ambition. To them, honor might win you the loyalty of your men or the admiration of the common folk, but it will prove useless when it comes to seizing power. In order to seize power, they believe that one must employ the practical, even the underhanded. Early on in the story, Jamie Lannister of the Kingsguard and brother to the Queen states "Give me honorable enemies rather than ambitious ones, and I'll sleep more easily by night."

# Family

Family is a very important concept in A Game of Thrones; loyalty to one's family is the keeps the Seven Kingdoms together. Each noble house constitutes one family; for example, anyone with the last name Stark would belong to Great House Stark. Smaller Houses serve and pledge fealty to these Great Houses, and all Houses, Great or small, ultimately pledge fealty to the King of the Iron Throne. During the course of the story, even devious or morally-corrupt characters display strong loyalty to their families. In a way, this is not unexpected, as there is an incentive for being loyal.

The Seven Kingdoms is a feudal society; therefore, being born into a noble family means enjoying all the privileges and power associated with one's family. By protecting the family, one is also protecting one's claim to that privilege and power; it is the rare man or woman who spurns the gifts they were born into. It is even in the family words of Great House Tully: Family, Duty, Honor. To the Tullys, the arrangement of those three words is important: duty and honor are important, but the family has to come first.

## Youth & Maturity

With the various battles and wars in the Seven Kingdoms, it is uncommon for one to live a long life. This is especially so for the common folk, who are often at the mercy of the noble houses and their game of thrones. Life in the Seven Kingdoms can be harsh; children grow up faster than they would in our world.

Boys born into nobility begin training as knights as early as 7 or 8, and girls as young as eleven can be betrothed to a boy not much older than themselves. A boy of 14 can even lead an army on the battlefield or be crowned King. These children take on responsibilities and duties that may seem unbearably heavy to us, but such is the way of life in Westeros.

## Adaptability

One of the themes often explored in A Game of Thrones is the change of one's destiny or dream. A lot of the younger characters are thrust into situations or surroundings which require them to change their worldview and childhood dreams – it is most often a rude awakening and each character copes differently.

Bran Stark, one of the main characters, hopes to be a great knight one day, but his dreams are dashed to pieces when he sustains serious injuries during a fall. His bastard brother, Jon Snow, dreams of being a ranger for the Night's Watch, but ends up a steward instead. Bran Stark's elder sister, Sansa Stark, wants her life to reflect that of the romantic songs she's heard over the years, tales that always come with handsome knights and beautiful ladies; she soon learns that life is not a song, and her worldview undergoes a dramatic shift as a result.

## Sex and Gender Roles

A Game of Thrones largely takes place in a medieval setting, where men rule and hold power. The eldest son always inherits the title and lands of his father; if he should meet an untimely end, the next eldest son claims the inheritance. Women can hold no land or castle; the role they play is limited to one of taking care of their husband's family and estate.

There are some women who struggle with these oppressive chains; they dislike being shackled by the expectations for their sex, and so try to navigate through Westerosi society in their own special way. Some do it subtly, keeping their femininity on the surface intact for the world to see, but who then plot and scheme behind closed doors, as power hungry as any ambitious man. Then there are those who do so in more direct and obvious ways, who strap on armor, wield sword and shield and engage their enemies on the battlefield alongside their male counterparts.

One of the main characters in the book, Arya Stark, has no wish to live the life of song and love that her elder sister, Sansa, dreams of; she sees marrying some noble lord and taking care of a family as a dream other girls long for, but it a dream that she has no desire for. Arya is far more interested in swordsmanship and exploration than she is in the traditional pursuits of femininity, but, because of her sex, she has never been given proper training, unlike her brothers who learned the arts of war and battle at a young age. Such is her tenacity and fiery temperament that her father eventually relents and hires a private instructor to teach her the ways of the sword.

# Character Overview

Main Characters

**Arya Stark**
**Brandon Stark**
**Catelyn Stark**
**Daenerys**
**Eddard Stark**
**Jon Snow**
**Robert Baratheon, King**
**Tyrion Lannister**
**Sansa Stark**
**Robb Stark**

Secondary Characters

**Barristan Selmy**
**Bronn**
**Cersei Lannister**
**Drogo**
**Gregor Clegane**
**Jaime Lannister**
**Jeor Mormont**
**Joffrey Baratheon**
**Jon Arryn**
**Jorah Mormont**
**Loras Tyrell**
**Petyr Baelish**
**Renly Baratheon**
**Samwell Tarly**
**Sandor Clegane**
**Stannis Baratheon**
**Theon Greyjoy**
**Tywin Lannister**
**Viserys**
**Varys**

# Main Characters

## Arya Stark

*Epithet: None*

*House: Stark*

Arya is Eddard and Catelyn's youngest daughter. While her sister
and brothers have inherited their mother's fair skin and auburn hair,
Arya takes after her father, with dark brown hair and a long and
solemn face. Her half-brother, Jon Snow, with whom she is very
close with, shares the same features, as well.

Arya has always envied Sansa's beauty and skill in the feminine arts
but considers her elder sister to be rather stupid, or at least, very
foolish. Arya Stark does have her own skills and talents, however:
she rides a horse well, and her quickness, agility and cunning have
often helped get her out of sticky situations. Out of all the Stark
children, she is the one that rebels the most against her destined role;
Arya does not see herself as a lady, to be married to some lord and to
look after her future husband's children and estate. No, that life is for
Sansa. Arya knows that her destiny is out there – she just has to find
it first.

# Brandon Stark

*Epithet: None*

*House: Stark*

Brandon Stark is Robb Stark's younger brother; he was named after his uncle, who was killed by the Mad King, Aerys II. He is more commonly referred to as "Bran" by his parents and siblings. Bran dreams of being a great and famous knight, standing at Robb's side. He is also optimistic, mentally strong and loves a good challenge; the men and women of Winterfell are used to seeing him scale the castle walls, scampering across old sections of the castle that no one has tended to in years. His mother constantly worries that he'll lose his footing one day; however, Bran has been climbing for years and has never once fallen. Bran is also gifted with unusually keen powers of observation.

# Catelyn Stark

*Epithet: None*

*House: Stark*

Catelyn Tully was originally betrothed to Brandon Stark; however, Brandon was killed by King Aerys II, an event that eventually led to the uprising that is now known as Robert's Rebellion. It was agreed that she then marry Brandon's younger brother, Eddard Stark. She has come to love Eddard over the years, and has given him five children.

The only point of conflict in their relationship would be over Jon Snow, the bastard Eddard sired, and brought back to Winterfell after Robert's Rebellion. Catelyn is the daughter of Lord Hoster Tully, head of Great House Tully. Lysa Arryn, wife to the late Jon Arryn, is her younger sister. Catelyn, like those from House Tully, value family, duty and honor over all other matters; she is very protective of her children and will go to the great lengths to mete out justice and punishment to those who dare harm them.

# Daenerys

*Epithet: Daenerys Stormborn*

*House: Targaryen*

Daenerys and her brother, Viserys, are the last of the Targaryens. She was born during Robert's Rebellion, after her father, King Aerys II, had been overthrown and killed. At that point in time, her mother and Viserys were in Dragonstone, the ancestral stronghold of the Targaryens. On the day of her birth, a ferocious storm struck Dragonstone, and thus she earned the epithet "Daenerys Stormborn". Her mother died giving birth to her, which makes her and Viserys the only living heirs of the Targaryen dynasty.

Both of them eventually fled to the Free Cities, where they have been wandering and living ever since. Daenerys is kind and gentle, and is afraid of her brother's cruel and spiteful streaks. She does, however, believe in his goal of reclaiming the Seven Kingdoms; like her brother, she believes that the Kingdoms rightfully belong to House Targaryen.

# Eddard Stark

*Titles: Lord of Winterfell, Warden of the North*

*House: Stark*

Eddard Stark, or "Ned" as he is affectionately known to his wife and close friends, is the head of Great House Stark. He resides in Winterfell, the ancestral home of House Stark; his rule extends over the vast provinces of the North. Eddard is a close friend to King Robert Baratheon, and played a major role in Robert's Rebellion. He is a very capable warrior; he uses his greatword "Ice" in battle and when dispensing justice in the North.

Honor is his greatest weapon, but many also consider it a chink in his armor: it instills loyalty in his men, but it also means that Eddard sometimes goes down the honorable path when it would be more advantageous and beneficial to take the practical and expedient path. And that is something his enemies look to exploit.

# Jon Snow

*Epithet: Lord Snow (only by brothers of the Night's Watch)*

*House: None*

In the North, all bastard children are given the last name of Snow. Some say that the men of the North are so full of honor that they bring their bastards into their family; this is exactly what happened with Jon Snow. No one knows who his mother is, save for his father, Lord Eddard Stark.

All everyone knows is that when Eddard went off to join Robert's Rebellion, he came back with a boy, his bastard son. He has told no one about the boy's mother, and even his good friend, King Robert Baratheon, is unsure of the mother's true identity. The fact that Eddard brought Jon Snow to live in Winterfell has long been a point of conflict between Eddard and his wife, Catelyn Stark. She has never hidden her dislike for him; Jon Snow knows this but leaves Catelyn well enough alone.

The fact that he looks so much like Eddard compared to Catelyn's true-born children must surely rankle, as well. Jon Snow is a quiet and thoughtful boy, very insightful for his age. He is also a talented swordsman.

# Robert Baratheon, King

*Titles: The First of His Name, King of the Seven Kingdoms*

*House: Baratheon*

Robert Baratheon led the rebellion against the Targaryens, overthrowing King Aerys II, the rule of the last Targaryen kings, to become the King of the Seven Kingdoms. In his youth, Robert Baratheon was a ferocious warrior, intimidating in stature and well-muscled; being King has taken its toll on him, and the Robert when the story begins is a fat king, prone to drinking and on the lookout for any diversions that allows him to escape his kingly duties.

Before the rebellion, he was betrothed to Eddard Stark's younger sister, Lyanna Stark. Lyanna, however, died during the rebellion. When he took to the Iron Throne, Robert married Cersei Lannister, as thanks to House Lannister for joining his cause. However, theirs is a loveless marriage, for even years after her death, he still pines for Lyanna.

# Tyrion Lannister

*Epithet: The Imp*

*House: Lannister*

Tyrion is the third child of Tywin Lannister. His entry into the world killed his mother, something his father has truly never forgiven him for. Tyrion looks nothing like this older siblings, Cersei and Jaime Lannister; the twins are well-known for their beauty, whereas Tyrion was born a dwarf, stunted and misshapen.

Knowing that only the power and prestige of House Lannister saved him from being thrown on out on streets to fend for himself, as would often happen with men and women born with his condition, Tyrion has taken to sharpening the one gift he has – a sharp and cunning mind. He has also built up a great deal of patience and tolerance, such that jibes and taunts about his height no longer bother him; in fact, he often makes self-deprecating jokes about his condition. Perhaps it is because of his experiences as a dwarf that Tyrion appears to deeply empathize with the plight of other social outcasts.

## Sansa Stark

*Epithet: None*

*House: Stark*

Sansa is the elder sister to Arya, a polite and gentle girl who is said to possess a beauty that surpasses her mother's. Unlike her sister's pragmatic approach to life, Sansa tends to veer towards the more fanciful: she wishes for her life to like the stories and songs, featuring chivalrous knights and beautiful princesses living happily ever after. She thinks her home, Winterfell, a boring place, where nothing ever happens. Upon hearing that she will be accompanying her father to King's Landing, Sansa is ecstatic with joy; she immediately begins day-dreaming of the numerous knights, ladies and tournaments that awaits her in the far more exciting capital.

# Robb Stark

*Epithet: None*

*House: Stark*

Robb Stark is Eddard and Catelyn's eldest son, making him heir to Winterfell and the North. He is close to all his siblings; due to their similar ages, he is also close to his half-brother, Jon Snow and Eddard's ward, Theon Greyjoy. Growing up as heir to his father's dominion, Robb has been trained in the ways of battle and military strategy; he has also been groomed for command, learning the arts of being an effective and inspiring leader. Like his father, he is just, honorable, and inspires loyalty and confidence in those who follow him.

# Secondary Characters

## Barristan Selmy

*Titles: Lord Commander of the Kingsguard*

*Epithet: Barristan the Bold*

*House: Selmy*

The Kingsguard are the King's elite bodyguards, seven knights who have vowed to serve and protect both the King and the royal family from harm – and they serve for life. The current roster of the Kingsguard leaves much to be desired, with the appointment of the current members appearing to be more about forging political ties rather than about selecting the very best knights in the Seven Kingdoms.

There was a time when the Kingsguard was exactly that – 7 knights chosen for their courage and skill-at-arms; these men were said to be the best warriors in all the lands, their legendary fighting prowess winning admiration from the small folk and nobles alike as well as instilling fear in the heart of the King's enemies.

Barristan Selmy came from such a time. He and Jaime Lannister are the only remaining Kingsguard that had served under King Aerys II; Barristan, severely wounded during Robert's Rebellion, was pardoned by Robert Baratheon and made Commander of the Kingsguard. Although he respects Jaime Lannister's bravery and skill, he is contemptuous of his fellow Kingsguard for killing the King he was supposed to protect. Even though he is currently in his advanced years, he is still a hale and hearty man, having lost none of his fearsome fighting abilities – he regularly takes part in tournaments with men who are far younger and almost always ends up at the top of the list.

## Bronn

*Epithet: None*

*House: None*

Unlike most of the characters in A Game of Thrones, Bronn is not of noble birth. He is a low-born sellsword, a man who works for the side that pays him the most coin; he'll do anything, kill anyone for the promise of gold and power. This often leads to high-born lords treating him with derision and contempt, but even they do not deny that Bronn is very, very good at his job.

The fact that he is still alive, given the nature of his job, is a good testament to his incredible martial prowess. He truly has no qualms about fighting dishonorably and will use every dirty trick and skill to come out on top in a fight. And in his line of work, that means being the last one standing.

# Cersei Lannister

*Titles: Queen of the Seven Kingdoms*

*House: Lannister*

Cersei Lannister is said to be one of the most beautiful woman in all the Seven Kingdoms; being the Queen to Robert Baratheon's King means that she also wields no small amount of power and influence. Add to that the fact that her father is Tywin Lannister, Lord of Great House Lannister, said to be the most powerful man in the Seven Kingdoms due to the size of his army, and you've got a woman who lives and breathes power and intrigue. She is a cunning player in the game of thrones, and she does her best to work against what she feels is the biggest restriction against her ambition: being born a woman. She loves her twin, Jaime Lannister, but has a far more restrained relationship with her young brother, Tyrion Lannister.

# Drogo

*Titles: Khal*

*House: N/A*

Drogo is a khal, the title the Dothraki give their chieftains. Thus he is often referred to as Khal Drogo by Dothraki and non-Dothraki alike. He became khal at a very young age, and his khalasar, or tribe, has grown to about 40,000 warriors, making it the largest horde on the Dothraki Sea, the vast grasslands where the Dothraki roam. Like all Dothraki warriors, he keeps his hair long. A Dothraki warrior only cuts his hair after he has been defeated in battle; Drogo's hair reaches the back of his thighs.

# Gregor Clegane

*Epithet: The Mountain that Rides*

*House: Clegane*

Gregor Clegane is Sandor Clegane's elder brother and currently the head of House Clegane. His epithet is due to his freakish size – he is almost eight feet tall, and almost all of that is pure muscle. Wielding a great sword larger than most men, while carrying a shield and wearing heavy plate armor, it's no wonder he's known as The Mountain by common-folk and nobles alike. His height gives him incredible reach, while his massive physical strength means that he can easily cleave a horse in two with his sword. Throw in his fiery temper and his cruel, brutal nature, and you have one of the most feared men in all the Seven Kingdoms.

# Jaime Lannister

*Epithet: Kingslayer*

*House: Lannister*

Jaime Lannister is Cersei's Lannister's twin brother, Cersei being older by only a handful of seconds. They share the same stunning good looks and have been each other's best friends since they were children. In addition to his comeliness, Jaime has also been blessed with a strong and quick body; his sense of balance, speed and natural talent make him one of the best knights in the Seven Kingdoms, easily defeating many taller and stronger men.

Jaime was raised to the Kingsguard when he was fifteen, becoming the youngest member in the history of the order. However, he is most known for slaying King Aerys II at the end of Robert's Rebellion, the very same King he had sworn to protect; he had been known as Kingslayer ever since. Jaime adores his twin, Cersei Lannister very much; he is also one of the few men in the Seven Kingdom who treats his younger brother, Tyrion Lannister, with genuine kindness and love.

# Jeor Mormont

*Titles: Lord Commander of the Night's Watch*

*Epithet: The Old Bear*

*House: None (previously of House Mormont)*

Jeor Mormont was once the head of House Mormont. When he was certain that House Mormont would be in capable hands, those of his son's, Jorah Mormont, he abdicated his seat and joined the Night's Watch. With his battle knowledge, wisdom and leadership skills, he quickly rose through the ranks, and now sits as Lord Commander of the Night's Watch. He deeply loves the Night's Watch; as Lord Commander, he sees the big picture and notices things the rest of his men often miss. And that is why he knows that, unless more men come to bolster the Watch's dwindling numbers, they might not be able to hold the wildlings and all the other dangerous creatures from North of the Wall at bay.

## Joffrey Baratheon

*Titles: Prince*

*House: Baratheon*

Joffrey Baratheon is Robert and Cersei's eldest son and heir to the Iron Throne. He is close to his mother but has a far more distant relationship with his father. Strong-willed and headstrong, Joffrey enjoys flaunting his privilege and power, knowing that being heir to the Iron Throne protects him from the repercussions of his actions. Joffrey has a cruel and sadistic streak, and a rather inflated sense of his own abilities – he loves to boast but seldom lives up to his claims. Despite all that, Joffrey is moderately charming, but only when he wants to be. He is most often seen accompanied by his sworn shield, Sandor Clegane.

# Jon Arryn

*Titles: Lord of the Eyrie, Defender of the Vale, Warden of the East, Hand of the King*

*House: Arryn*

Jon Arryn fostered both Robert Baratheon and Eddard Stark at the Eyrie, and he came to love them as his own children, just as they came to love him as a second father. When King Aerys II demanded that Jon hand over both boys to the King's justice, Jon Arryn rebelled; House Stark and House Baratheon followed shortly thereafter. His marriage to Lysa Tully forged an alliance with House Tully. The marriage was largely loveless, but Lysa eventually gave him an heir, Robert Arryn, named in honor of Robert Baratheon. At the story of the story, Jon Arryn, the Hand of the King, is just recently deceased; he seems to have died under mysterious circumstances.

# Jorah Mormont

*Epithet: Jorah the Andal*

*House: Mormont*

The Dothraki call him Jorah the Andal, due to the fact the middle-aged knight comes from Westeros. He was once the Lord of House Mormont, a vassal family of the Great House Stark. His father, Jeor Mormont, decided to leave House Mormont's only holdings, Bear Island, to Jorah, whom he deemed as capable.

Jeor Mormont went on to join the Night's Watch while Jorah took over as Lord of House Mormont. In order to pay off some debts, he sold several captured poachers into slavery. When Edward Stark learned of this, he immediately headed to Bear Island to dispense the King's Justice (for slavery is illegal in the Seven Kingdoms, punishable by death). Jorah knew that if he were to meet Eddard, he would be given only two options: death, or joining his father in the Night's Watch. He chose a third option: exile. The disgrace he has inflicted on his house still weighs heavily in his heart, and he hopes that one day, he might receive a pardon and be able to return to Westeros.

# Loras Tyrell

*Epithet: The Knight of Flowers*

*House: Tyrell*

Loras Tyrell is the youngest son of Lord Mace Tyrell, head of Great House Tyrell and one of the most powerful men in the Seven Kingdoms. Loras once squired for Renly Baratheon, but is now a knight in his own right — and a very good one at that. Despite being only sixteen, he displays considerable skill at arms, but especially so in the joust. Beautiful, chivalrous, clad in the very finest of armor and helm, and with a knack of knowing how to put on a mesmerizing show for the crowd, Loras Tyrell is every bit the knight in shining armor, plucked right out from a song.

# Petyr Baelish

*Titles: Master of Coin*

*Epithet: Little Finger*

*House: Baelish*

Petyr Baelish is also known as Littlefinger, not because of the size of his actual fingers, but because he is a very minor lord, his only holding being located on the smallest of 'The Fingers', the rocky area on the shores of the Vale of Arryn.

In his childhood, he was fostered at Riverrun, where he fell in love with Catelyn Tully. When Catelyn Tully was betrothed to Brandon Stark, Petyr challenged Brandon to a duel. Catelyn knew of Petyr's love for her, and though she did not love him the way he loved her, she begged Brandon to spare Petyr's life. Brandon acquiesced to her wishes; he easily won the duel, but left Petyr with a scar on the chest. Petyr now works on the King's small council, his financial acumen standing him in good stead as the council's Master of Coin. He is very intelligent and ambitious, and is a master at court intrigue.

# Renly Baratheon

*Titles: Lord of Storm's End, Master of Laws*

*House: Baratheon*

Renly Baratheon is King Robert Baratheon's youngest brother. He currently sits on the King's small council as the Master of Laws. Tall, well-built, and handsome, Renly has always been said to look like a younger version of Robert. Even Eddard Stark, Robert's best friend, finds the similarity eerie.

Renly tends to cut a striking figure wherever he goes, not only because of his similarity to his brother, but because he is often dressed up in only the most fashionable and finest of clothing and armor. He is also extremely charismatic: he makes friends easily and his men are incredibly loyal to him, even bordering on zealotry. However, his easy nature and tendency to make jokes even in the most dire of circumstances can sometimes come across as being flippant and irreverent.

# Samwell Tarly

*Epithet: None*

*House: None (previously of House Tarly)*

Samwell Tarly is the eldest son of Lord Randyll Tarly, widely considered to be among the best military commanders in the Seven Kingdoms. To Randyll's dismay, Samwell grew up to be a gentle-hearted boy who had no interest in military affairs or in being a knight – the boy was intelligent, well-read and perceptive, but hated the sight of blood. Sam's mother eventually gave birth to another boy, one that was robust and fierce-spirited, a child much more to Randyll's liking.

From then on, Randyll would devote almost all of his time to Sam's younger brother. And then one day, Randyll gave his eldest son a choice: either join the Night's Watch, or be "accidentally killed" in a hunting accident. Both choices would lead to the same conclusion: with Sam out of the picture, Randayll's youngest son would be his heir, who, in his mind, was far more suitable to take over House Tarly compared to Sam. And so Samwell Tarly "chose" life over death, and headed for the Wall, alive but afraid what the Night's Watch has in store for him.

# Sandor Clegane

*Epithet: The Hound*

*House: Clegane*

Sandor Clegane is Prince Joffrey's personal bodyguard. He is often referred to as "The Hound", partly because he belongs to House Clegane, whose sigil is three black dogs on a field of yellow, but more likely it is due to his very distinctive helm, forged and shaped into the form of a snarling dog's head.

There are extensive burn marks on the left side of his face; that plus his towering height and martial prowess, often gives him a menacing demeanor. He is often contemptuous of knights and the whole idea of knighthood; his animosity towards his brother, Gregor, a knight who appears to have no qualms about murdering and killing innocent people, appears to be the reason behind his contempt.

# Stannis Baratheon

*Titles: Lord of Dragonstone, Master of Ships*

*House: Baratheon*

Stannis Baratheon is the elder of King Robert Baratheon's younger brothers. While Renly is all smiles and charm, Stannis is the exact opposite; a hard and unyielding man, Stannis considers even the smallest slight to his honor as a personal attack, to be dealt with as swiftly as possible. His stubborn determination in the face of adversity and overwhelming odds was never more on show than during Robert's Rebellion, where he successful held Storm's End against a siege led by a much bigger army – they say that when the food ran out, Stannis survived on rats and boiled leather.

Stannis sits on the King's small council, as the master of ships, but when A Game of Thrones begins, it appears he has hastily left King's Landing for unknown reasons. Upon digging deeper into the mystery of Jon Arryn's sudden death, Eddard learns that both men had been spending a great deal of time with each other before Jon's untimely death. Since neither Jon nor Stannis has been particularly close to each other, the question then becomes why.

## Theon Greyjoy

*Epithet: None*

*House: Greyjoy*

Theon Greyjoy is the heir to Pyke, the ancestral home of Great House Greyjoy. House Greyjoy staged a rebellion against King Robert Baratheon's rule a few years after Robert was crowned King; though they had some victories, the Rebellion was eventually crushed by King Robert and Lord Eddard Stark.

The head of House Greyjoy, Balon Greyjoy, was allowed to remain the overlord of the Iron Islands; however, his only surviving son, Theon, was sent to Winterfell, as a hostage and ward to Eddard Stark. Theon has grown up with the Starks, and despite being a hostage to ensure his father's good behavior, he has been treated very well by Lord Eddard and the Starks. He treats Robb Stark as a close friend, but does not get along well with Jon Snow.

Theon has a streak of arrogance in him, but for the most part, it does not surface too often. He is a skilled archer and takes great pride in his ability to make incredibly accurate shots.

# Tywin Lannister

*Titles: Lord of Casterly Rock, Warden of the West, Shield of Lannisport*

*House: Lannister*

Tywin Lannister is not a man anyone wants for an enemy. As the head of the Great House Lannister, Tywin is probably the most powerful man in all of the Seven Kingdoms: the King's court owes House Lannister a huge sum of money, his daughter is Queen, and, due to the resource-rich Lannister lands and his shrewd handing of money, Tywin is easily the richest man in all of Westeros. And it is because of Tywin's immense wealth that the Lannister army is the best equipped force in the Seven Kingdoms. At the end of Robert's Rebellion, Tywin sacked King's Landing and order the execution of Prince Rhaegar Targaryen's wife and children; the years have not made him any kinder.

# Viserys

*Epithets: Beggar King*

*House: Targaryen*

Viserys styles himself as the Lord of the Seven Kingdoms, but men in the Free Cities call him the Beggar King, due to his constant requests for military aid to help him secure the Iron Throne. When his brother, Rhaegar Targaryen, was slain by Robert Baratheon on the Trident, Viserys became heir to the Targaryen dynasty He and his sister, Daenerys, are the last remaining Targaryens. Viserys never refers to Robert Baratheon by name; he only refers to Robert as 'The Usurper'. He plans to one day lead a huge army back to the Seven Kingdoms, to claim what he deems as rightfully his – the Iron Throne. Just how he plans to achieve this remains a mystery to his sister, since Viserys has no fortune, nor ever handled a sword in battle. He treats Daenerys, well enough, but can show a cruel streak when he loses his temper (which is often); he often refers to his outbursts as 'waking the dragon', and uses them as a threat to get Daenerys to do his bidding.

# Varys

*Titles: Master of Whisperers*

*Epithet: The Spider*

*House: None*

Varys sits on the King's small council, as the Master of Whisperers, acting as the King's spymaster. He is one of the very few characters in A Game of Thrones who does not hail from Westeros; he has hinted at spending some time in the Free Cities in his early youth, but with Varys, one can never tell whether the things that come out from his mouth are truth, half-truths, or outright lies. What is known about him is that he is a eunuch, and is incredibly good at his job. He is also known as The Spider, due to his intricate web of informants (whom he refers to as "little birds") that stretch out across Westeros, and even across the Narrow Sea.

# Main Settings

## Braavos

On the northernmost tip of the eastern continent (Essos), lies Braavos, arguably the most powerful of the nine Free Cities. Braavos is ruled by the Sealord, and has close ties to Pentos, one of the other Free Cities located further south on the western coastline of the continent. Braavos consists of approximately a hundred or so islands, separated by water, and linked together by bridges.

They are a seafaring people, and their warriors, called bravos, are famous for their unique style of swordsmanship, known as Water Dancing. The style eschews armor, and makes use of slim, narrower blades; it also focuses more on precise footwork and agility rather than hacking and slashing. This style probably arose because of the danger of wearing armor onboard a ship.

# Casterly Rock and the Westerlands

The Westerlands consists of numerous hills and valley and falls under the rule of Great House Lannister. Although the region is small compared to those held by the other Great Houses, it is rich in precious metals, and it is largely this, and Lord Tywin's business skills, that have made House Lannister the richest House in all the Seven Kingdoms. The Lannister rule from their ancestral home, Casterly Rock, a stronghold carved into a mountain, said to be one of the most heavily-defended castles in the Kingdoms.

# Dragonstone and the Crownlands

The Crownlands is an administrative region directly under the control of the Iron Throne. It consists of the capital, King's Landing, and all nearby surrounding areas. This control also stretches to the nearby islands and the ancient fortress of Dragonstone. Both the island and the fortress itself are referred to by the same name.

The keeps and towers of this massive fortress take the form of ferocious dragons, for this stronghold was once the ancestral home of Great House Targaryen. After he overthrew the Targaryen dynasty, Robert Baratheon made the elder of his younger brothers, Stannis Baratheon, the Lord of Dragonstone.

# The Eyrie and The Vale of Arryn

The Vale of Arryn is located on the south east of the Neck, on the east coast of Westeros. It is surrounded on all sides by the Mountains of the Moon, and, as the name implies, it falls under the rule of Great House Arryn. They Arryns rule the Vale and the surrounding lands from their ancestral home, the Eyrie.

The Eyrie is thought to be impregnable because of its location: it sits atop a very high mountain, and to get to it, one would have to pass through three waycastles. And after the last waycastle, Sky, there are only two ways to continue the ascent: by sitting in a basket pulled up by six winches, or by foot, on a very narrow trail.

While it would seem foolish to call any fortress unassailable, it would certainly be an incredibly difficult endeavor for any army to take the Eyrie by force. Savage mountain clansmen can also pose a danger to smaller parties travelling to the Vale; these mountain clans have been plaguing the knights of the Vale for years, but due to the poor quality of their weapons, they pose little threat to a large party of armed knights or hired sellswords.

# The Fingers

Much of the Vale of Arryn's broken coastlines stretch out into long, thin fingers, pointing outwards towards the Narrow Sea. Much of the land here is rocky and barren, with the soil being very stony and sandy, making it exceedingly difficult to grow food along the Fingers. The seat of House Baelish, a very minor House with only one member (Petyr Baelish), sits on the smallest of the Fingers, which is how Petyr came to be known as 'Littlefinger'.

# Harrenhal

Not far north from King's Landing is a huge lake, known simply as God's Eye. And on the northern shores of the lake sit Harrenhal, a massive castle made completely from black stone. Harrenhal is the biggest castle in Westeros; an entire army can fit into the great hall.

The castle was built by Harren the Black, who boasted that it was impregnable – Targaryen dragons proved that claim false, burning Harren to a crisp while he was safely ensconced in his massive castle. Over the years, the castle has changed hands several times, and has earned a rather sinister reputation for being cursed, as past owners and their Houses often seem to experience a bad series of events, often leading to mysterious and inexplicable deaths.

# Highgarden and The Reach

The Reach is blessed with the most fertile plains and grasslands in all of Westeros, and is ruled by Great House Tyrell, from their ancestral home in Highgarden. Due to the amazing fertility of the land, the Reaches is the most populated region in the Seven Kingdoms, and as such, they have the largest army out of the all the Great Houses.

Highgarden is said to be a beautiful stronghold; the Reach is also home to Oldtown, the second most populated city in the Seven Kingdoms, but said to be more beautiful than King's Landing, with none of the stench or dirtiness of the capital.

# The Haunted Forest

This is the name given to the forest just north of the Wall. It is a very extensive forest, stretching for hundreds of miles. The dense foliage provide cover to wildling parties wishing to make their way around the Wall, and it for this reason that the Night's Watch always work to ensure that the forest stays clear of the Wall itself, lest a wildling attack catches them unawares.

Due to their limited manpower, however, they are only able to do this immediately north of the three occupied castles. So far, only small wildling raiding parties have used the forest as cover, but recently, disturbing reports of strange, alien creatures in the Haunted Forest have begun to surface.

# King's Landing

The most populous city in Westeros, King's Landing is the capital of the Seven Kingdoms, located on the east coast, overlooking Blackwater Bay. It was founded by Aegon Targaryen, the founder of the Targaryen dynasty.

The city is built around three hills. On Rhaenys' hill sits the Dragonpit, where the Targaryens once kept their legendary dragons. Visenya's hill sports the Great Sept of Baelor. The Red Keep, which holds the King's Iron Throne, sits atop Aegon's Hill. While King's Landing may indeed be home to a great amount of people, many have noticed that there is a strange stench to the city, and that it isn't particular clean or beautiful.

# The Neck and Moat Cailin

Anyone attempting to enter the North from the South, on land, has to go through the marshy swampland known as The Neck. And in the Neck sits Moat Cailin, a ruined fortress consisting of three intact towers, the first line of defense against any southern army. To reach the North, the invading army has to pass through Moat Cailin – there is no way to bypass it the army travels by land. And since the ground is not firm enough for the deployment of siege weapons, that means that the invading army will be exposed to missile fire from archers stationed amongst the three towers – it is said that a hundred or so archers can hold off an army many, many times its own size.

# Pentos

Pentos is one of the nine Free Cities on the continent of Essos. It is located on the west coast of Essos and is a major seaport. The major merchant lords of Pentos control the rich and bustling city, and because its location makes it vulnerable to Dothraki invasions, the merchant lords often ply the Dothraki with gifts and lavish parties in order to appease them.

# Pyke and the Iron Islands

The Iron Islands is one of the smallest regions of the Seven Kingdoms, consisting of seven islands off the western coast of Westeros, northwest of Riverrun. Those who live here are known as Ironmen, a tough and ferocious people, with a long history of raiding and pillaging the coastline. Land on the islands is stony and thin, making it difficult for the Ironmen to grow much food.

There is also a lack of resources – when combined, these two factors explain why the people of the Iron Islands are much poorer than their mainland counterparts. The Iron Islands are under the rule of Great House Greyjoy, from their ancestral stronghold of Pyke, on the island of the same name.

# Riverrun and the Riverlands

The Riverlands is located in the middle of Westeros, and is an extremely fertile land due to the many rivers that run across its expanse. It has been conquered more than a handful of times in the past, but it is presently under the rule of Great House Tully. Riverrun is the ancestral home of the Tullys, and it comes with a unique defensive mechanism: sluice gates can be open to flood a channel on the west side of the castle, turning Riverrun into an island. An invading army wanting to hold Riverrun at siege would have to separate their army into three different parts to place them around the castle in order to prevent supplies and reinforcements from coming in.

# Storm's End and the Stormlands

The Stormlands are located south of King's Landing, on Westeros' east coast, so named due to the frequent storms that rage all over the coastline. The region is home to large stretches of thick forest, and the land is generally damp and wet. Great House Baratheon rules the Stormlands from their ancestral home, Storm's End, a tower of gigantic proportions surrounded by a massive wall.

This formidable stronghold has never fallen in battle; the story of how Stannis Baratheon managed to hold Mace Tyrell's siege for over a year during Robert's Rebellion, surviving only on rats and boiled leather, is now legendary.

# Sunspear and Dorne

Dorne refers to the southernmost part of Westeros; it is a region of mountains and deserts, with fertile land being all along the rivers. The weather can get quite hot in Dorne, and the people take after the weather, being fiercely protective of their passions and principles. Dorne falls under the rule of Great House Martell, who keeps watch over the land from their ancestral home, Sunspear, a stronghold with sand-colored walls.

# The Twins

As per the name, the Twins are a pair of castles, fortified and connected by a bridge that spans the Green Fork River. The Twins are the ancestral home of House Frey, and they have grown very wealthy over the years by charging a toll to those who wish to cross. And there are quite a few good reasons to cross; parties from the North that intend to head to Riverrun can save themselves several days of journeying by crossing the Twins, while those that travel from Riverrun with the intention of heading North almost always cross the Twins in order to avoid the swampy marshland of the Neck. The head of House Frey, Lord Frey, a prickly old man with progeny in the double digits, determines the toll, depending on the party intending to cross; the payment isn't always gold.

# Vaes Dothrak

The Dothraki only have one city – Vaes Dothrak. It serves as both capital and religious city. It is located under the shadows of a vast mountain known as the Mother of Mountains. The Dothraki do not build; the statues of deities in the city belong to cities that the Dothraki have conquered, now long since dead and left in ruins. Likewise, all the strange buildings littering the streets were built by the slaves that the Dothraki brought back with them to Vaes Dothrak.

The city is large enough to hold all the Dothraki tribes, but under normal circumstances, the only souls in the city are the dosh khaleen, the wives of former tribal leaders, and the eunuchs and slaves that serve them.

# The Wall

A colossal wall of ice that stretches across the northern border of the Seven Kingdoms, the Wall is said to be built by, Brandon the Builder, thousands of years ago. It acts as the first line of defense against the uncivilized and barbaric wildlings that live north of the Wall. The order that defends the Wall is known as the Night's Watch.

They occupy three castles along the length of the wall: Castle Black in the middle, which serves as their headquarters, The Shadow Tower in the far west, and Eastwatch by the Sea, along the far eastern shoreline. There are nineteen castles along the length of the Wall, but due to a lack of manpower, only the aforementioned three are occupied and maintained, with the remaining castles having long since collapsed or been left in ruins.

The Night's Watch might be dwindling in numbers, but still they sit diligently at the Wall, protecting the Seven Kingdoms from invasion by, not only wildlings, but the other strange, feral creatures of the Far North.

# Winterfell and The North

Winterfell is the ancestral home of Great House Stark and from where the Starks rule over the North, a vast but sparsely populated expanse of land that is almost always covered in a blanket of white due to the endless amount of snow, even during the summer. The people of the North, commonly referred to as "northmen", are a hard, stoic people, with many of them believing that the blood of the First Men still flows in their veins. Further up North is the Wall, home of the Night's Watch.

# The Dothraki Sea

In the interior, of the eastern continent (Essos) is the Dothraki Sea, a vast expanse of grassy plains and steppes. The Dothraki Sea is so named due to the fact that the grass grows thick and tall, and this causes the entire landscape to look like a sea of gentle, rolling waves when seen from afar. It is home to the Dothraki, a nomadic horse-riding people, widely-feared for their skill at arms. Even experienced commanders in the Seven Kingdoms acknowledge the dangers of going head-to-head with the Dothraki on an open field.

# Chapter Summary

# Prologue

Three rangers from the Night's Watch are chasing after wilding raiders in the Haunted Forest. One of them scouts ahead and discovers a clearing, where he comes across an eerie scene: the wildling raiders appear to have been killed in their sleep, but there is no sign of blood anywhere. He returns to the other two and leads them back to the wildling's campsite, but when they arrive, the bodies are gone.

They inspect further, but during their inspections, strange, milky, translucent and alien creatures, called Others by the Night's Watch, enter the clearing, and proceed to slay the rangers. One ranger is killed in battle while another one is killed while trying to escape; the third ranger managers to flee.

# Chapter 1 – Bran

Lord Eddard Stark and his household guards, along with his eldest son (Robb Stark) middle son (Bran Stark), bastard (Jon Snow) and ward (Theon Greyjoy) ride to one of the nearby holdfast near Winterfell, to execute a man for deserting the Night's Watch (the ranger who manages to escape in the Prologue).

Lord Eddard Stark dispenses justice, beheading the deserter with his greatsword, Ice, forged from Valyrian steel. On their way back to Winterfell, they discover a dead direwolf, killed by a stag's antlers, a bad omen since the direwolf is the sigil of Great House Stark, while the Stag is the sigil of Great House Baratheon, the King's House. They discover 6 direwolf pups, and Eddard allows his kids to have it. One of the direwolf pup is an albino and given to Jon Snow.

# Chapter 2 – Catelyn

Catelyn visits the godswood, a forest in the middle of the Winterfell, where there is one heart tree. The First Men worshipped the old gods, and it is said that the blood of the First Men flow in the Starks and the Northmen. Catelyn is uncomfortable with the godswood, because she worships the Seven, like most of those from the South. She finds Eddard Stark cleaning Ice at the heart tree. Eddard tells her of the deserter, and that his brother Benjen Stark, First Ranger of the Night's Watch, has been telling him that the order has seen more deserters of late.

Catelyn tells Eddard that she has received a letter from King Robert Baratheon, revealing that the Hand of the King, Jon Arryn, has died of a sudden mysterious illness. Eddard is sad because he and Robert were fostered in the Vale under Jon Arryn. Catelyn informs Eddard that the King will be coming to Winterfell, along with his whole entourage, which includes the Queen, Cersei Lannister, and their children. Ned is uneasy, as he always felt that the Lannisters rallied around Robert's Rebellion a little too late.

# Chapter 3 – Daenerys

Viserys gifts Daenerys with a fine silk dress, telling her that it was the gift from Illyrio Mopatis, their host in Pentos. Viserys tells Daenerys that he will be presenting her to Khal Drogo, a horselord who has the largest khalasar (host of horse-warriors), and who is renowned for never having been defeated in battle.

Daenerys, Viserys and Illyrio head over to Khal Drogo's manse, a huge structure with nine towers. In the party, they spot Ser Jorah Mormont, an anointed knight who fled the Seven Kingdoms due to selling some poachers to slave traders, an illegal act in the Seven Kingdoms. Illyrio eventually brings Khal Drogo over to meet Daenerys.

# Chapter 4 – Eddard

King Robert Baratheon and his 300-strong entourage arrive. Eddard almost does not recognize the King because the last time he saw Robert was over nine years ago, and Robert has gotten fat. The Queen and her children are also introduced to the Starks. Robert and Eddard then descend into the Stark family crypt.

Down in the crypt, the King and Eddard head over to pay respects to Eddard's father and older brother, both killed by the last Targaryen king, Aerys II. They also pay their respects to the Eddard's sister, Lyanna Stark, who died during Robert's Rebellion; she had been betrothed to Robert Baratheon at the time.

Robert then shares with Eddard the sudden death of Jon Arryn, and how Jon Arryn's wife, Lysa, has fled to the Vale with her son. Robert then requests that Eddard be the new Hand of the King; he also requests that Eddard's eldest daughter, Sansa Stark, be wed to his own son, Prince Joffrey. Eddard does not want the position, but Robert insists; Eddard mentions that he'll have to think about it.

# Chapter 5 – Jon

The welcome feast for the King is a merry affair, with all the Stark children in attendance. The Stark children sit with their parents, in the high seats, while Jon Snow sits in the common area. He is surprised and happy to meet his uncle, Benjen Stark, Lord Eddard Stark's brother and First Ranger of the Night's Watch.

Benjen wonders aloud why his brother appears to be in a somber mood tonight. Jon states that it might have something to do with Lord Eddard bringing King Robert to the Stark family crypts, which he had noted, angered the Queen. Benjen praises Jon's powers of observation and states that the Night's Watch could use men with Jon's skills at the Wall. Jon, having drunk quite a lot, asks Benjen to take him to the Wall when the feast is over. Benjen states that Jon might be still too young for the Wall. Jon does not take kindly to this and leaves, going outside whereupon he meets Tyrion Lannister. The two exchange words and Tyrion even gives Jon some advice on how to avoid being hurt by insults.

# Chapter 6 – Catelyn

Catelyn and Eddard are in bed, discussing Robert's offer. Eddard states his reluctance to take the King up on his offer, but Catelyn tells him he must, lest the King query his loyalty. During their discussion, Maester Luwin, advisor to the Stark house, comes in with a letter, written in code.

Catelyn recognizes the code – it is a code created by her and Lysa, her sister and the late Jon Arryn's widow, when they were young girls. In the letter, Lysa tells Catelyn that her late husband was murdered by the Lannisters, with this being the reason why she has left King's Landing and fled to the safety of the Vale. Catelyn implores Eddard to take up the King's offer, because as the new Hand of the King, he can unravel the mystery behind Jon Arryn's death. Eddard agrees, and tells Catelyn he will bring Sansa, Arya and Brandon to King's Landing. Robb will remain at Winterfell, while Maester Luwin tells Eddard that Jon will be heading to the Wall to join the Night's Watch.

# Chapter 7 – Arya

Arya is doing needlework along with Sansa and Princess Myrcella, under the watchful eye of Septa Mordane. Septa Mordane criticizes Arya's needlework in front of everyone, and feeling frustrated at the thought of never being as beautiful or as skilled in the feminine arts as Sansa, Arya flees to the courtyard instead, where she sees her brother, Bran, sparring with the King's youngest son, Prince Tommen.

There she also meets up and chat with Jon Snow – the two are very close, and the only they possess the dark hair and long facial features of their father (as opposed to the other children, who, with their red hair and pale skin, take after Catelyn). A verbal spat takes place between the Lannisters and the Starks when the master-at-arms of Winterfell, Rodrik Cassell, refuses Prince Joffrey's request to duel with Robb Stark using real swords. The Lannisters then leave, with Joffrey taunting Robb as he leaves.

# Chapter 8 - Bran

Bran is happy that his father has decided to take him to the capital, King's Landing. While the King and most of the men from the castle are off for their final hunt, Bran decides to go around the castle to bid farewell to everyone. However, he finds the whole thing unbearably sad, so he takes to his favorite activity: climbing the castle walls. Bran has always been a good climber--he has never fallen.

While climbing an old abandoned tower, he overhears a man and a woman having sex through one of the windows. He climbs closer and hears the woman worrying about Eddard Stark going south with them to King's Landing; she is afraid that Eddard is plotting against the Lannisters as he has never shown any interest in going south. The man seems calm about it, stating that he'd rather face an honorable man like Eddard Stark rather than the King's brothers, Renly and Stannis. The woman screams when she sees Bran at the window. Bran realizes that it is the Queen, Cersei Lannister, and the man is Jaime "Kingslayer" Lannister, the Queen's brother. Jaime pushes Bran off the window ledge.

# Chapter 9 - Tyrion

Tyrion spends most of the night reading, unable to go to sleep due to the constant howling of a direwolf (Bran's) in the Stark castle. He decides to go have breakfast and encounters Prince Joffrey with his personal bodyguard, Sandor Clegane, also known as "The Hound" due to his helmet resembling a snarling dog's head.

Tyrion tells Prince Joffrey to pay his respects to Lord Eddard, adding that the Prince's absence has been noted. Prince Joffrey initially refuses, but after several hard-fisted slaps from Tyrion, scampers off to do Tyrion's bidding. Tyrion then goes for breakfast, where he meets his sister, Cersei, and his brother, Jaime. Cersei has never liked Tyrion, but Jaime has always treated his brother kindly.

Tyrion tells them that Maester Luwin thinks Bran Stark is going to live, at which point Cersei and Jaime exchange a quick look. Tyrion notices this but mentions nothing. He tells his siblings that he is going to the Wall, and that he very much hopes Bran will eventually awaken.

# Chapter 10 - Jon

Jon visits Bran, who has fallen into a coma, to wish his final farewells. Catelyn Stark is in the room; she has never left Bran's side since the fall. It is revealed that Catelyn hates Jon due to the fact that he is Eddard's bastard and the fact that Eddard brought Jon back to Winterfell to grow up with their trueborn children.

Jon then leaves to say goodbye to Robb and Arya. He surprises Arya with a sword forged by Mikken, the Stark's smith and armorer. The sword's blade is a bravos' sword: thin, slender, and pointed – not so good for slashing, but great for piercing. Both Jon and Arya agree that the sword's name is Needle.

# Chapter 11 – Daenerys

It is Daenerys' wedding feast, held just outside of Pentos, in the open, with tens of thousands of people attending (mostly Dothraki). Khal Drogo sits next to Daenerys, but ignores her for the whole feast. Ser Jorah Mormont, having sworn fealty to Viserys, brings books on the Seven Kingdoms as his gift to Daenerys. Viserys offers her 3 handmaidens (all three provided by Illyrio, since Viserys has no money).

Illyrio gives Daenerys 3 petrified dragon eggs. The feast is wild, involving mass orgies and more than a handful of deaths. At the end of the feast, Khal Drogo presents his gift, a beautiful silver horse. Finally, Khal Drogo leads Daenerys away from the feast, to a small stream. Though she is very much afraid at first, she is surprised by Khal Drogo's sensitivity and gentle caresses, and the two eventually make love.

# Chapter 12 – Eddard

One morning, on their way to King's Landing, Eddard and King Robert have a private chat. Robert shows Eddard a letter received by Lord Varys, the Master of Whisperers on the King's small council. It is a letter from Ser Jorah Mormont, informing Varys of the marriage between Daenerys Targaryen and Khal Drogo. Eddard Stark remembers Jorah Mormont; the knight brought shame to the North when he tried to sell several captured poachers to slave traders.

Meanwhile, Robert has decided to name Jaime Lannister, Warden of the East, a title that has traditionally gone to the Arryns. Eddard cautions Robert against this, saying it'll put too much power in the hands of the Lannisters. He also tells Robert a story the King has never heard before: that during Robert's Rebellion, when Eddard went to King's Landing to claim the Iron Throne for Robert, he found Jaime sitting on the throne, with the dead King's (Aerys II) blood on his sword. Jaime treated the whole thing like a joke, but Eddie had been mistrustful of the man's trustworthiness ever since. Robert is unconcerned and sticks to his decision.

# Chapter 13 – Tyrion

Jon, Ghost and Benjen Stark are on their way to the Wall, along with Tyrion and two of his personal servants. On the way, they are joined by another Night's Watch brother, Yoren, who is bringing two rapists from back to the Wall. Jon questions Tyrion about his habit of reading books.

Tyrion answers that his intelligence are one of the few gifts he was born with, and like how his brother Jaime keeps his sword sharp, so too must he keep his mind sharp. Jon claims that the Night's Watch is a noble calling, but Tyrion tells him otherwise – that the Night's Watch is a place where all the misfits of the Seven Kingdoms go: rapists, poachers, peasants, bastards and the like. Jon ultimately concedes that Tyrion has the truth of the matter.

# Chapter 14 – Catelyn

Maester Luwin enters Bran's room one night; the young boy is still in a coma and Catelyn has been at his side since the fall. Maester Luwin implores Catelyn to go through the accounts with him and, since Eddard took a large retinue of men to King's Landing, assist him with appointing new men to the now-empty household positions. Luwin's request makes Catelyn angry, but Robb steps in to diffuse the situation, offering his assistance to Maester Luwin instead.

The two men suddenly notice a fire going on outside, and rush off to help put it out. Catelyn walks to the window to look out, only to suddenly realize that a strange man is in the room with her, holding a knife. The man is surprised at Catelyn's presence; he had expected Bran to be left unguarded. They struggle, and Catelyn suffers deep cuts to her fingers due to the sharp blade, but Bran's direwolf comes to the rescue, killing the man.

After several days of sleeping and healing, Catelyn wakes up and calls together a small council consisting of Robb, Theon, Maester Luwin and Rodrik. The council comes to the conclusion that the man was hired to kill Bran due to the large sum of money they found on his body, as well as the fine knife the man carried. Catelyn reveals her suspicions, that the Lannisters were behind the death of Jon Arryn, and that it must have been Jaime Lannister who pushed Bran. Her evidence: Jaime had not having gone to the hunt. The council agrees that Catelyn and Rodrik will go to King's Landing to find the truth behind the Valyrian steel knife – they go by ship.

# Chapter 15- Sansa

Sansa meets the two men who have ridden from King's Landing to join the King's entourage. Barristan Selmy is the Commander of the Kingsguard, a select group of knights whose duty it is to protect the King. Renly Baratheon is Robert Baratheon's younger brother. She also meets Ser Ilyn Payne, the King's mute executioner.

Ser Ilyn Payne scares her but Sansa quickly forgets her distress when Joffrey invites her to a day of riding with him. They ride, explore the land and have lunch together. They then come across Arya Stark using wooden sticks to practice her swordplay with her friend, Mycah, the butcher's boy. Joffrey taunts Mycah with his princely sword, and is about to do hurt the butcher's boy when Arya intervenes, hitting Joffrey with her wooden stick. Joffrey retaliates, but Arya's direwolf, Nymeria, savages the arm of the Prince, who then falls to the ground whimpering. Arya throws the Prince's sword into the nearby river and runs off.

Sansa tries to help the injured Prince, but he treats her with scorn. Sansa rides off to find help.

# Chapter 16- Eddard

Eddard is furious that Arya was brought before the King by Lannister men, before he even had a chance to talk to her. Queen Cersei seeks justice for what has happened to her son. Joffrey tells everyone that Arya and the butcher's boy had ambushed him, struck him with their wooden sticks and set Nymeria upon him.

Arya, incensed at the Prince's outright lies, sticks to telling the truth. Sansa is then brought in to tell her story: she lies, telling everyone she did not remember what happened. Arya is furious. The Queen seeks punishment. King Robert agrees to discipline Joffrey if Eddard will discipline Arya, which Eddard agrees to only too willingly. Cersei is not satisfied, and requests that the direwolf that attacked Joffrey be slaughtered. Since Nymeria has disappeared, Cersei points to Sansa's direwolf, Lady, as a replacement. King Robert agrees, much to Eddard's dismay. Eddard is angry, but he refuses to let Lannister men kill Lady; he offers to do the deed himself. And he does.

The Hound returns, with the body of Mycah; he tells Eddard that the boy had run, but not fast enough.

# Chapter 17 - Bran

Bran is dreaming; he is falling. As he falls can see the Seven Kingdoms, as well as the mysterious lands to the East. He is afraid of falling because he knows he'll die if he doesn't stop falling. A three-eyed crow tells him to fly, because it was the only way for him to avoid death. Bran tries, and much to his delight, manages to soar. The crow starts to peck at Bran's forehead, between his eyes, and that is when Bran wakes up, with his direwolf on the bed with him.

When Robb bursts into Bran's room, Bran tells him that he now knows his direwolf's name: Summer.

# Chapter 18 – Catelyn

Catelyn and Rodrik finally arrive at King's Landing, before the King's party. They take a room at an inn. Rodrik goes off to find the Ser Aron Santager, the King's master-at-arms, hoping that the man would know the owner of the Valyrian steel knife. Not long later, City Watch guards come to escort Catelyn; they take her to Petyr Baelish, more commonly called "Littlefinger", who was once enamored with Catelyn Stark when they were children and who now holds a position on the King's small council. Lord Varys, the King's Master of Whisperer, also known as "The Spider", joins the meeting as well, asking to see the dagger; Catelyn complies. Petyr immediately recognizes the knife – he reveals that it is his. He had lost it in a wager – he tells Catelyn that he had backed Jaime Lannister in a joust, while Tyrion had backed Loras Tyrell. Loras Tyrell has unhorsed Jaime, and the knife went to Tyrion.

# Chapter 19 – Jon Snow

Jon is trying to adapt to life on the Wall. Ser Alliser Thorne, the master-at-arms at Castle Black, oversees the recruits' training. Jon manages to best all the other Night Watch recruits. However, Ser Alliser Thorne only has scorn for Jon and the other new recruits; he creates nicknames for each of them, and calls Jon "Lord Snow", a cruel poke at Jon for being a bastard.

Jon gets into a fight in the armory with several other recruits, but Castle Black's blacksmith, Donal Noye stops them before the fight gets serious. Jon tells Donal that the other recruits hate him because he is better than them. Donal reveals the truth: that they actually hate him because he is a bully. Jon protests but Donal points out Jon's privilege of having been trained by a very competent master-at-arms at Winterfell; in contrast, some of the recruits are only holding a sword for the very first time. Jon concedes the point, and leaves, ashamed of his attitude towards the other recruits.

Tyrion accidentally bumps into Jon, and they chat for a while about Jon's uncle, Benjen Stark, who has not yet returned from a ranging trip. Jon is then summoned to see Jeor Mormont, the Lord Commander of the Night's Watch. Jeor, or "The Old Bear" as he is known to the brothers of the Night's Watch, hands over a letter written by Robb – the letter states that Bran is alive, although he has forever lost the use of his leg. Jon is happy that Bran is alive, and runs to the mess hall to celebrate with Tyrion. He is so happy that, in an attempt to make amends with the other recruits, offers to show them how to improve their form and swordsmanship. Ser Alliser mocks him, but Jon returns the barb in kind, leaving Ser Alliser fuming.

# Chapter 20 – Eddard

Eddard arrives in King's Landing and is immediately summoned to convene with the King's small council. He is joined by Littlefinger, Varys, Renly, and Grand Maester Pycelle. There are two other members who sit on the council, but Stannis Baratheon, the elder of King Robert's younger brothers, has returned to Dragonstone, while Ser Barristan is with King Robert.

The small council announces that there is to be tournament, in honor of Eddard's appointment as the new Hand of the King. Eddard balks at this, especially when he learn just how much the crown is in debt, with a significant portion of that debt being to House Lannister.

After the meeting, Littlefinger takes Eddard to a brothel to meet his wife. Eddard is surprised that Catelyn is in King's Landing but listens to the story she tells him, of the man who tried to kill Bran, and of the Valyrian steel knife belonging to Tyrion. Eddard promises to search for evidence on the Lannisters' involvement in the hired killing. He then instructs Catelyn and Rodrik to return to Winterfell and make preparations for a possible war. Littlefinger, because of his love for Catelyn, agrees to help Eddard find Jon Arryn's killer.

# Chapter 21 – Tyrion

After dinner, Tyrion and Jeor Mormont have drinks together.
Mormont begs Tyrion, who is heading off to King's Landing, to help
him find more men for the Night's Watch. Mormont knows that
Tyrion's father, Lord Tywin Lannister, is one of the most powerful
men in the realm, one with a very large army. Mormont recounts the
reports he has heard from the other two castles on the Wall
(Eastwatch and the Shadow Tower), of strange things happening
North of the Wall. Tyrion is embarrassed that the Commander has
asked for his help, but he promises to help the Night's Watch cause.

Tyrion then walks up to the top of the Wall, for one last look. He
meets Jon and Ghost there. Jon tells him that he's starting to make
friends with the other recruits. Tyrion states that he will be stopping
at Winterfell on his way to King's Landing. Jon pleads with Tyrion,
hoping that Tyrion can help Bran. Tyrion says he'll try to help Bran
the best he can. The two part way as friends.

# Chapter 22 – Arya

Eddard has dinner with his daughters and tells them of the
tournament being held in his name. Sansa is delighted at the idea of
attending a tournament, but Arya is still despondent about the death
of Lady and Mycah. Arya eventually leaves dinner, angry that no
one so much as mentions Mycah and runs to her room. Her father
eventually comes, and they have a heart-to-heart talk. He sees her
holding Needle, and asks about the sword.

Arya reveals that Jon gave it to her. She then reveals that she feels guilty about Mycah's death, but Eddard tells her that it is not her fault. He also states that there must be no dissension among the Starks because being in King's Landing, they are now amongst many enemies. He allows her to keep the sword. The next day, she meets Syrio Forel, a very skilled Braavos swordsman; Eddard has hired Syrio to teach Arya how to handle a sword.

# Chapter 23- Daenerys

It has not been easy for Daenerys: the many days or riding and Drogo's lovemaking at night has made her almost suicidal. However, one night, she dreams of being purified and cleansed by dragonfire. After experiencing this dream, she becomes stronger, both in body and mind, and begins to enjoy her new life as Drogo's wife.

Khal Drogo's khalasar is riding at the edge of the Dothraki Sea. She orders her party to stop, and walks into the grasses of the Dothraki Sea, admiring the beauty of the land. Viserys stomps into the clearing, furious that Ser Jorah had the temerity to tell him to leave her alone. One of Daenerys' bodyguards stops him by coiling a whip against his neck. As Viserys lies on the ground, Daenerys looks at him with pity. She then instructs her bodyguard to let him go, but she orders his horse taken away from him, which is a great insult to a horse-loving people like the Dothraki. She and Jorah have a chat, both agreeing that Viserys would make a terrible King.

When they make camp, Daenerys notices that the petrified dragon eggs are warm to the touch. One of her three handmaidens teaches her how to better pleasure the Khal. That night, Drogo and Daenerys make love; he is surprised by her request to be on top, but their lovemaking session is more passionate than ever. When they reach the far side of the Dothraki Sea, Daenerys realizes she is pregnant.

# Chapter 24- Bran

The nanny, or "Nan", is reading stories to Bran when Maester Luwin comes in with news that Tyrion Lannister has arrived in Winterfell. Nan's great-grandson, Hodor, a man nearly seven-feet in height, carries Bran to the great hall. In the hall, Robb sits as head of House Stark. Tyrion asks whether Bran remembers anything about the fall but Bran says he doesn't.

Tyrion then hands over a special gift to Bran: the design of a custom-made saddle that would allow Bran to ride a horse. Robb apologizes for his earlier rudeness and offers Tyrion and his men a place to stay for the night at Winterfell, but Tyrion refuses, choosing instead to stay at a nearby brothel. Yoren, a member of the Night's Watch that is accompanying Tyrion to King's Landing, accepts the invitation. During dinner, Yoren tells Robb of Benjen Stark's disappearance. After the dinner, Robb meets Bran in his room, and they both commiserate over the unfortunate state of affairs they now find themselves in.

# Chapter 25- Eddard

Lord Eddard meets with Grand Maester Pycelle. Eddard learns from Pycelle that Jon Arryn had come to Pycelle, looking for a book; Jon falls ill the very next day. Eddard suspects Jon Arryn could have been killed by poison, but Pycelle is not convinced since in the Seven Kingdoms, poison is thought to be the weapon of cowards and women. Pycelle also tells Eddard that before his death, Jon Arryn whispered something to the King: "The seed is strong."

Lord Eddard then questions Pycelle on the Queen's whereabouts during Jon's illness and eventual death; Pycelle tells him that the Queen was journeying to Casterly Rock, the ancestral stronghold of House Lannister, to escort her father to King's Landing. Eddard leaves with the book: it is an old tome, about the genealogies of the various Houses of the Seven Kingdoms.

Littlefinger visits Eddard's chambers. He informs Eddard that he has discovered that four members of Jon Arryn's household still remain in King's Landing. One of them is Ser Hugh of the Vale, Jon's squire, knighted after Jon's death. Eddard is interested in speaking to this newly-knighted squire, but Littlefinger advices Eddard to send a man from his household instead, a man he trusts. Littlefinger explains that this is because spies are everywhere in King's Landing and from the window, he points out several of the Queen's and Lord Varys' spies, seemingly going about that their work, but at the same time keeping an eye out for all that transpired around them.

# Chapter 26 – Jon

Jon is getting along with most of the new recruits. There is a new recruit to the Night's Watch: a fat boy by the name of Samwell Tarly. Ser Alliser mocks Sam, and the new boy gets beaten up in a mock fight. Jon jumps to his protection, however. After the fight, Jon and his new friends ask why Sam refused to fight: Sam reveals that he is a coward.

Sam eventually shares his story with Jon: he was his father's eldest son and heir, but his father considered him unsuitable to take over as head of House Tarly. His father wanted to get rid of Sam so that he could instead appoint Sam's younger brother as his rightful heir. Sam was given a choice: Join the Night's Watch, or be "accidentally killed" in a hunt.

Jon tells the other recruits not to hurt Sam in training. Everyone agrees except a recruit named Rast. Jon uses Ghost to wake up a sleeping Rast, a threat that elicits an agreement. From that day on, none of the recruits go after the new boy, and Sam eventually falls in with them.

# Chapter 27 – Eddard

Eddard's men go out to find and question the four members of Jon Arryn's household still in King's Landing. The newly-knighted squire, Ser Hugh, refuses to answer any questions. The rest gave them two clues: before his death, Jon and Stannis Baratheon had been seen together, visiting a brothel and an armorer's shop. Eddard sends some of his men to search for the brothel while he heads out to the armorer's shop.

Upon arriving at the shop, he discovers that Jon and Stannis had been inquiring about an apprentice armorer. Within several minutes of talking with the young, sturdy boy, who had blue eyes and thick black hair, Eddard realizes that he is talking to one of King Robert's bastards. He leaves the shop wondering why Jon and Stannis had been doing the exact same thing.

# Chapter 28 – Catelyn

Catelyn and Rodrik, on their way back to Winterfell, stop at an inn for the night. Catelyn wonders what to do next. She mulls a bit and comes up with two choices. One is to travel to Riverrun to warn her father of the dangers of a possible war. The other is to travel to the Vale, to confer with her sister, Lysa Arryn, about the truth behind Jon's death. She eventually decides that heading back to Winterfell would be a safer choice.

By a stroke of coincidence, Tyrion pops into the same inn, accompanied by his two servants and the Black brother, Yoren. Acting on impulse, Catelyn, with the help of the other patrons of the Inn who turn out to be loyal to her father and House Tully, takes Tyrion captive. She announces that she will be bringing Tyrion back to Winterfell to await the King's justice.

# Chapter 29 –Sansa

Sansa is enjoying the tournament. Only four riders remain in the
joust: Sandor Clegane, Gregor Clegane, Jaime Lannister and Ser
Loras Tyrell. Gregor Clegane actually killed one of the knights he
rode against, the tip of the lance spearing the knight in the neck. The
winner will be decided the next day.

There is a feast that night, and Prince Joffrey finally talks to her
again; he had remained withdrawn after the incident with Arya and
Mycah. At the end of the feast, he asks Sandor to escort her back to
her chambers. The Hound is drunk and mocks Sansa's love for
knights and romantic fairy tales. He shares the story behind the ugly
burns on his face: when they were children, Gregor punished Sandor
for stealing a favorite toy by pushing his face against a brazier. He
then warns her not to repeat the story to anyone else, threatening to
kill her if she does so.

# Chapter 30 – Eddard

Eddard and Ser Barristan converse over the body of the dead knight,
killed the day previously by Gregor Clegane in the joust – it is Ser
Hugh of the Vale, Jon Arryn's recently knighted squire. Eddard then
goes into the King's tent and convinces Robert not to join the melee
competition, stating that no men would want to hit the King.

The joust continues: Jaime Lannister loses to Sandor Clegane. In the joust between Gregor and Loras Tyrell, Gregor's stallion starts to become unruly and wild. Gregor is unhorsed by Loras. Furious at his loss, Gregor kills his stallion and proceeds to attack Loras until he is stopped by his brother, Sandor. The two Cleganes fight until the King orders them to stop. Petyr Baelish explains to Sansa the reason Gregor's stallion was distracted: Loras's mare was on heat.

Back in Eddard's chambers, Lord Varys meets with Eddard. He reveals that the Queen had intended for Robert to die in the melee. Varys allies himself with Eddard and reveals that Jon Arryn was indeed killed by poison, the untraceable Tears of Lys. When Eddard inquires to the reason behind Jon's murder, Varys replies that it was because Jon had been asking questions.

# Chapter 31 – Tyrion

Tyrion is surprised that Catelyn isn't taking him to Winterfell, but to the Vale of Arryn instead. He had been hoping that someone at the inn would bring news of his capture to his father, but now sees that Catelyn's announcement at the inn was a ruse, to draw off any Lannister attack.

Catelyn tells Tyrion that she knows the Valyrian steel knife belongs to him, and she recounts Littlefinger's tale to him, of how Tyrion had won the knife betting against his brother, Jaime. Tyrion is about to defend himself when the entire group is ambushed by a gang of mountain clansmen. They win the battle but suffer 3 losses. In the fight, Bronn, one of the hired sellswords accompanying them to the Eyrie, fought particularly well.

After the battle is over, Tyrion tells Catelyn why Littlefinger's account of the wager was wrong: Tyrion would never bet against family.

# Chapter 32- Arya

Syrio Forel has set Arya the job of catching cats. While running after a cat, she finds herself in a strange section of the castle, where the skulls of the once famous Targaryen dragons are kept. She overhears a conversation between two men, who talk in whispers about how the Starks and Lannisters would soon be at war, and how the khal wouldn't do anything until his son is born.

Arya hears a lot of other things, but she understands little of it. Eventually, she makes her way out of that part of the castle and runs to tell her father of what she has just heard. Eddard appears concerned but doesn't take her story seriously. Yoren then arrives in the Hand's Chambers; in a private meeting, Eddard learns from Yoren that Catelyn has now taken Tyrion Lannister prisoner.

# Chapter 33 – Eddard

The King's small council convenes, will all members presents save Stannis Baratheon. Varys presents an important piece of news: Daenerys Targaryen is pregnant. King Robert wants to send an assassin to kill Daenerys. Eddard argues against doing this, and he is backed up by the ever-honorable Barristan Selmy. However, all the other members of the council agree with the King's proposal. Seeing that Robert is not about to budge, Eddard resigns as Hand of the King.

Eddard is packing up, having ordered his guards to gather all his household members in preparation for their departure back to Winterfell, when Petyr Baelish enters his chambers. Petyr tells Eddard that the King has decided to give a lordship to any man that successfully kills Daenerys. Petyr also tells Eddard that he has discovered the brothel that Jon Arryn and Stannis Baratheon had visited together. He suggests that they both visit the brothel before Eddard heads back to Winterfell.

# Chapter 34 – Catelyn

Catelyn and her party are attacked by another group of clansmen; 3 more men die. They approach the first of the Vale's gates, and Catelyn continues on foot alone, in the darkness. It is normally dangerous, but Lysa Arryn has requested that her sister meet her immediately. She completes the dangerous journey, finally arriving at the ancestral castle of the Arryns, the Eyrie. When she finally comes face-to-face with her sister, she learns that Lysa is furious at her for bringing Tyrion to the Vale.

Lysa wants her son, the sickly Robert Arryn, to stay in the Vale. Her reason: before his death, Jon Arryn had told her that "the seed is strong". Lysa interprets this as Jon referring to their son, Robert Arryn. Catelyn warns Lysa that even the Eyrie is not impregnable. Robert Arryn then mentions that he wants to see Tyrion "fly", a euphemism for throwing someone down the mountainside. Lysa Arryn muses that the Arryns might just do that to Tyrion.

# Chapter 35 – Eddard

Eddard, Petyr and several Stark guards head over to the brothel which Jon Arryn and Stannis Baratheon allegedly visited. They meet another one of the King's bastards, a baby girl win fine dark hair. When Eddard asks whether Jon Arryn was killed because he knew about Robert's many bastards, Petyr says the notion is preposterous, considering that Robert's many bastards around the Seven Kingdoms isn't exactly a secret.

As they leave the brothel, they are surrounded by Jaime Lannister and a party of Lannister guards. Petyr runs off, promising to bring the City Watch. Jaime demands for Tyrion's release, threatening to kill Eddard for ordering his brother's capture. Eddard warns Jaime that doing so would make Tyrion a dead man. Jaime reluctantly agrees and rides off, telling his guards to kill all of Eddard's men but to leave Eddard alone. Eddard helps his men, but they are badly outnumbered. He falls from his horse and breaks a leg; his men are slaughtered. He is brought back to the castle, where Maester Pycelle administers to his serious wound.

# Chapter 36 – Daenerys

Daenerys and the rest of the khalasar enter Vaes Dothrak, capital and the holy city to the Dothraki. Khal Drogo intends to make a sacrifice in the city. Daenerys and Ser Jorah talk about the chances of a Dothraki army invading the Seven Kingdoms. Jorah mentions that Viserys is quickly losing patience, but states that Khal Drogo will offer his help in good time.

Daenerys invites Viserys to dinner, with the hope of giving him some fine Dothraki garments. Viserys, in his pride, mistakes this for an order, and threatens her. She hits him, and warns him that should he threatens her again, she would have him killed. Daenerys hugs one of the dragon eggs to sleep that night and falls into slumber knowing that the son in her belly would be the true king, the true Targaryen dragon.

# Chapter 37 – Bran

Bran goes out on his first ride, using the special saddle that was created for him based on Tyrion Lannister's design. He is accompanied by Robb, Theon and some of the household guards. Their direwolves go along as well, hunting for prey in the forests. Bran is enjoying his ride but during the ride, Robb tells him of their father's encounter with Jaime Lannister in King's Landing, and how he had been injured and the rest of the men killed. Upon hearing this, Bran feels sad and wants to return to the castle, but they have to go off to look for their direwolves first.

While doing so, Bran is ambushed by a gang of six – four being deserters of the Night's Watch, and the other two wilding women. Robb, Theon and the direwolves come to the rescue, and in the ensuing skirmish, only one of the wildling women, Oshawa, survives. She is taken back to Winterfell for questioning.

# Chapter 38 – Tyrion

Tyrion finds himself in a cell. The cells in the Eyrie are not like other cells: one can always escape, by jumping down the mountainside. Tyrion eventually manages to bribe the brutish gaoler into taking him to Lysa Arryn. He tells the gaoler it is because he wishes to confess his crimes, but instead, he requests for a fair trial. When told he would be trialed by the sickly Robert Arryn himself, Tyrion declines to take part in the farce and says he wants a trial by combat. Lysa chooses Ser Vardis, an honorable knight, to be her champion. Tyrion chooses his brother, Jaime, but his choice is rebuffed by Lysa, who says that Jaime is too far away and that the trial would begin today. Tyrion looks around him in despair, but is relieved when Bronn volunteers to be his Champion.

# Chapter 39 – Eddard

Eddard is finally awake after a week of sleep and rest. The King and Queen immediately visit him in his chambers. The King is angry over the whole affair. Eddard asks the King to give him leave to go capture Jaime, who has since fled King's Landing to return to Casterly Rock. The Queen accuses Eddard of seizing her brother, Tyrion, an action which started everything. Robert tells Eddard to release Tyrion and make peace with Jaime. Cersei insults Robert for not agreeing with her, and Robert responds by hitting her. Cersei leaves. The King leaves shortly thereafter for a hunt, but before leaving, he reappoints Eddard as the Hand of the King.

# Chapter 40 – Catelyn

The trial by combat between Ser Vardis and Bronn takes place. Ser Vardis is fully armored and enters combat with a shield; Bronn enters with very light armor, and declines the offer of a shield. The two men fight, and Bronn's strategy quickly becomes apparent to several of the onlookers: to evade Ser Vardis' attacks, and let the weight of the heavy plate armor and shield slowly take its toll upon the knight's strength and speed. The strategy is successful, and Bronn manages to kill Ser Vardis. Lysa unwillingly frees Tyrion, and his belongings are returned to him. He is also given horses and supplies. Tyrion and Bronn depart from the Eyrie.

# Chapter 41 - Jon

A bunch of new recruits arrive at Castle Black, so Ser Alliser decides to elevate Jon and some of the other recruits to full members of the Night's Watch. Jon is happy, but quickly realizes that Sam would have a horrible time now that Jon wasn't there to protect him. Jon mulls over the problem then makes a visit to Ser Jeor Mormont's adviser, Maester Aemon. He begs the Maester to convince Commander Mormont to raise Sam to the rank of a full member, as well. When asked why, Jon says that every man has a role to play, and that while Sam might be useless as a fighter or ranger, he is intelligent, has good eyes, knows how to read and with those qualities, he'd be able to help the Maester with some of his chores. Aemon tells Jon he will think about it.

# Chapter 42 – Tyrion

On their way down the Eyrie, Tyrion convinces Bronn to stay by his side with the promise that "A Lannister always pays his debts". Tyrion has already shown that he keeps his word; before leaving the Eyrie, he gave all his gold pieces to the Arryn's brutish gaoler. When they make camp for the night, a band of mountain clansmen sneak up upon them.

Tyrion and Bronn are hugely outnumbered. The mountain clansmen are about to kill the two interlopers, but Tyrion successful persuades them to let the both of them go by promising them steel weapons and armor, of which the Lannister have plenty of. He tells the mountain clansmen that after he's supplied them with weapons and armor, they will then be able to take control of the Vale.

# Chapter 43 – Eddard

King Robert, Prince Joffrey and Renly are out hunting, so Eddard
sits on the Iron Throne, dispensing justice. A group of knights from
the Riverlands pleads their case, accompanied by peasants and small
folk who tell of raids against three Riverlands holdfasts. The
peasants tell of the destruction done by the group of raiders, led by a
man of humongous size.

Eddard and the knights realize that the leading the raiders is none
other than the Mountain, Gregor Clegane. Eddard denounces and
attaints Gregor, stripping him of all his titles and lands, and
sentences him to death. Ser Loras Tyrell begs Eddard for the honor
of leading the party against Gregor, but Eddard gives it to a young
lord, Beric Dondarrion.

# Chapter 44 – Sansa

Eddard informs both his daughters that they were going back to
Winterfell. Arya is unhappy about this and wants her father to bring
Syrio Forel along. Sansa is far more distraught, pleading with her
father to let her stay on in King's Landing. She declares her love for
the Prince and says that she will give him a son with bright, golden
hair, the exact same color as Prince Joffrey's. Sansa's words catch
Eddard by surprise; he realizes her words are the last clues to
mystery of Jon Arryn's death.

# Chapter 45 – Eddard

Sansa's words made everything clearer: when Eddard checks the genealogical book, the one that Jon Arryn had gone through, he discovers that Baratheons always have black hair. The book lists several pairings of Baratheons with Lannisters, and in each and every one of the pairings, the offsprings had black hair. Jon Arryn's words "The seed is strong" is referring to this, that all true Baratheon children have black hair. Eddard confronts the Queen privately, exposing her secret. She admits, without any shame, that yes, Prince Joffrey, Prince Tommen and Princess Myrcella are all Jaime's children, not Robert's. Eddard warns Cersei that he will be revealing her secret to the King and advices her to flee before the King comes back. Cersei is not afraid of Eddard's threat, however, and she says that he should be the one fearing her wrath.

# Chapter 46 – Daenerys

In Vaes Dothrak, Daenerys takes part in a religious ceremony. She finishes eating the raw heart of a stallion; the old crones declare Daenerys' son 'the stallion who mounts the world'. She names the child Rhaego, after her elder brother, Rhaegar Targaryen, killed by Robert Baratheon during Robert's Rebellion.

A feast is held. Viserys makes a scene at the feast; he is drunk and insulted that Drogo placed him at the back of the tent. Viserys draws his sword, even though Jorah has told him that no blood can be spilled inside Vaes Dothrak. He threatens Daenerys, stopping only when Khal Drogo finally agrees to give Viserys a crown. Viserys smiles, but is immediately grabbed by the Khal's guards. Drogo proceeds to 'crown' Viserys – with a pot of molten gold. Viserys dies, and Daenerys casually remarks that her brother was no dragon, since true dragons cannot be killed by fire.

# Chapter 47 – Eddard

The King has returned from the hunt -– and he is dying. Drunk during the hunt, he had missed his thrust against the boar; the boar then gored him and ripped him to shreds. Robert, seeing death at his doorstep, has a heart-to-heart talk with Eddard; he regrets sending assassins against Daenerys, and tells Eddard to stop them if he can. He also writes a letter, one that names Eddard as Lord Regent and Protector of the Realm until his heir comes of age.

Eddard assigns one of his men to take Sansa and Arya onboard the ship he has chartered to sail his daughter back them to Winterfell. He also hands the man a letter, to be brought to Stannis Baratheon, urging the elder of Robert's younger brother's to sail to King's Landing to claim the Iron Throne.

Petyr then arrives, and warns Eddard not do to this as that would surely ensure war with the Lannisters. He offers his help to Eddard, to rule as Regent until Joffrey comes of age, but Eddard says that the throne rightfully belongs to Stannis, for Joffrey and the other children are not Robert's children. He instructs Petyr to ensure that the City Watch is on his side when he faces the Queen.

# Chapter 48 – Jon

Jon, Sam and several of the recruits are raised to the Night's Watch and assigned into different orders. To his shock and surprise, Jon is assigned to the stewards. He is angry and blames Ser Alliser for keeping him out of the rangers, an order Jon believes he will excel at due to his martial prowess.

Sam placates Jon, telling him that his assignment as the Lord Commander's personal steward was requested by the Commander himself; the reason being that Mormont wants to groom Jon to be his successor. Jon is ashamed of his outburst. The two of them go to take their vows in a heart forest, in front of the old gods. Ghost returns to the clearing, and shocks everyone with the human hand it carries in its jaws.

# Chapter 49 – Eddard

King Robert is dead. Eddard is summoned to the throne room. He brings Petyr and Janos Slynt, Commander of the City Watch, along. In the throne room, Prince Joffrey orders the small council to prepare for his coronation. Eddard reveals the letter that names his as Lord Regent and Protector of the Realm.

Cersei reads the later but then rips it to shreds. Cersei declares Joffrey the rightful King. Eddard proclaims Stannis Baratheon as the rightful heir to the Iron Throne. Joffrey then orders the Lannister guardsmen to kill Eddard. Eddard commands the City Watch to take the Queen and her children into custody. The City Watch turns on Eddard instead, killing his men. Eddard is betrayed by Petyr, who shoves a dagger under his chin.

# Chapter 50 – Arya

Arya is training with Syrio Forel when five Lannister guards and Ser Meryn, one of the Kingsguard, confronts them; they insist on bringing Arya to her father. Syrio is instantly suspicious and tells Arya not to go with them. A fight ensues, one in which Syrio defeats all five guards, but Ser Meryn, fully-armored, manages to chop Syrio's wooden sword in half. Arya flees the scene.

She heads to the stables, and to her horror, sees the dead bodies of Stark household guards; they had been preparing her things for the trip back to Winterfell has been killed by Lannister guardsmen. She manages to find Needle, but is forced to kill a stableboy in the process. She then flees into the castle, down the secret passageway she had discovered the other day.

# Chapter 51 – Sansa

It is revealed that Sansa told the Queen of her father's plans, in the hope that the Queen would stop them, which would result in Sansa not needing to return to Winterfell; she does this because she loves Joffrey. After several days, Sansa is taken to meet the Queen, who informs her that her father is a traitor who wanted the Iron Throne for himself. The Queen then convinces Sansa to write letters to her mother and her elder brother, Robb Stark, telling them to come to King's Landing to swear fealty to Joffrey.

# Chapter 52 – Jon

The men at Castle Black have discovered two corpses; one has a hand missing (the hand that Ghost found previously). The corpses are identified: they are members of the Night's Watch. Sam notices that the bodies are not decomposing, even though it appears that men have been dead for quite some time. The men also note another eerie detail: both of the dead men have blues eyes, but both men were not blue-eyed when they had been alive.

The news that the King is dead has reached Castle Black. Mormont informs Jon that his father has been arrested and charged with treason. Everyone seems to know this, as well. Ser Alliser taunts Jon, and Jon attacks, but is restrained by his friends. Mormont is disappointed in Jon and sends him to the cells.

Jon wakes up and hears Ghost scrabbling at his door. The guard is dead. Heading over to the Lord Commander's chambers, he is horrified to discover one of the corpses inside – walking upright. Jon engages the wight in battle. The wight appears to be unstoppable; even dismemberment doesn't seem to stop it. Ghost attacks the wight, taking its attention off Jon. When Mormont comes out from his room with a lantern, Jon grabs the lantern, burning his hand in the process, and throws it at the drapes. He then throws the burning drapes on top of the corpse.

# Chapter 53- Bran

The Stark's bannermen arrive at Winterfell, to answer Robb's call. Some of them think he is not ready, some try to flatter him with gifts. One, Greatjon Umber, even draws his weapon in front of Robb, but Robb's direwolf, Grey Wind, swiftly deals with the big man, biting two of his fingers off. After that incident, Greatjon becomes Robb's staunchest supporter.

Bran goes to the godswood to pray. He notes that the youngest Stark child, Rickon, has been acting strangely of late, going into the Stark family crypts with his direwolf, Shaggydog. Osha, the wildling survivor, now working as a kitchen staff at Winterfell, chances upon Bran in the godswood. She tells him that she been trying to warn Robb that he was going in the wrong direction; that instead of heading South, he should be marching North to face the others. But Robb did not listen.

Robb, Theon and the Stark bannermen head south two days later.

# Chapter 54 – Daenerys

Daenerys tries to convince Drogo to conquer the Seven Kingdom, but he states that he has no interest in doing so at the moment. To take her mind off this, Ser Jorah suggests that Daenerys and her party go to visit the markets, as a great caravan just arrived. She does, and after arriving at the market, Jorah splits from the group, to see whether he has received any letters from Illyrio.

A wine merchant tries to sell his wares to Daenerys. When he learns her true identity, he offers her a special cask of wine, the very best from the Arbor. Jorah rejoins the party. He is suspicious of the wine merchant and demands that the merchant drink from the special cask, in front of them. The wine merchant pretends to do so but then tries to run away. He doesn't get far as Daenerys' bodyguards catch him before he can flee.

Jorah then tells Daenerys that Illyrio sent him a letter, informing him that King Robert Baratheon has offered a lordship to any man who kills Daenerys and her son. When they return to camp, Daenerys thrusts her dragon eggs into a burning brazier, but nothing happens. When Drogo hears of the assassination attempt, he becomes incensed and promises to conquer the Seven Kingdoms for his son.

# Chapter 55 –Catelyn

Catelyn has now left the Vale, and on her way back to Winterfell, she chances upon Robb's army at Moat Cailin. Robb shows her the letter from Sansa; Catelyn reads the letter and tells him the letter is a threat from Cersei.

Robb updates her on the situation: Jamie Lannister and his army are laying siege to Riverrun, while Tywin Lannister is leading another army on the opposite side of the river, catching Beric Dondarrion's group (the one in charge of executing Gregor Clegane) by surprise, and killing everyone in the group, although there have been rumors that Beric managed to escape.

Robb then tells her his plan: to send his foot soldiers to meet Tywin, while his cavalry forces will ride hard and fast down the other side of the river in order to free Riverrun from Jaime Lannister's siege. Robb wants his mother to go back to Winterfell, but Catelyn tells him she fears for her brother and father in Riverrun so she will go with him.

# Chapter 56 –Tyrion

Tyrion come across his father's army; it is at the very inn where
Tyrion had been taken prisoner by Catelyn. He learns all that has
happened so far, how Jamie was successful in surprising Riverrun
and how Tywin managed to destroy almost all of Beric Dondarrion's
forces, although Beric himself escaped. The clansmen, led by Bronn,
burst into the meeting; Tyrion introduces them to his father. A
messenger comes in with news that Robb Stark's army is riding
down the causeway, towards Tywin's army. Tywin invites the
clansmen to join in the attack. They agree, but only if Tyrion rides
with them.

# Chapter 57 – Sansa

Joffrey is now King. He has Grand Maester Pycelle read off a list of
nobles who must come to King's Landing to swear fealty to him.
Among these are Stannis and Renly Baratheon, the Tyrells, Lord
Frey, Catelyn Stark and all of the Stark children (except Sansa).
Joffrey then names his grandfather, Tywin Lannister, as the new
Hand of the King. Janos Slynt, the Commander of the City Watch, is
given a lordship and Harrenhal for siding with the Lannisters instead
of Eddard Stark.

Ser Barristan Selmy is stripped of his title as Commander of the
Kingsguard; he is replaced by Jaime Lannister. Upon hearing this,
Barristan is filled with anger and contempt, rejecting Cersei's offer
of a nice piece of land, and throws his sword at the King's feet
before leaving.

Sansa then pleads to Joffrey to show mercy to her father. Joffrey looks on and tells her that he will, if Eddard will confess to plotting against him. Sansa is relieved because she knows her father will do exactly that.

# Chapter 58 – Eddard

Eddard is in the dungeons, his injured leg giving him much pain. He flits between wakefulness and sleep. When he sleeps, he dreams of his younger years, of Robert's Rebellion.

After days have passed, a gaoler enters Eddard's cell; he is surprised to see that it is Lord Varys in disguise. Varys tells Eddard that Cersei will be down to see him the next day, and advices Eddard to confess his crimes, order Robb to lay down his arms, and proclaim Joffrey as the true King. Eddard refuses to do so, but Varys warns him that Sansa might pay the price for his decision.

# Chapter 59 – Catelyn

Robb Stark and his army need to cross the Twins. The Twins are controlled by House Frey, and the bridge is the only available option if they want to cross the Green Fork of the Trident. Doing so will mean they can race ahead to deal with Jamie Lannister, without needing to go through Tywin Lannister. They have been killing spies and ravens, to avoid Tywin catching wind of their plans.

Catelyn enters the Twin to speak to Lord Walder Frey and ask his permission to cross the Twins. Walder is rude to her, but she persists, and they eventually come to an agreement: Robb and his army can cross, as long as Robb takes on one of Walder's sons as a squire and marries one of Walder's daughters. Catelyn relays this to Robb who is not keen on the idea, but agrees to it anyway. Robb and most of his men cross the bridge, leaving Lord Roose Bolton to lead a small detachment to continue south to keep Tywin's army occupied.

# Chapter 60 - Jon

Jon Snow's right arm is been badly burned due to throwing the fiery drapes down upon the wight, but it is slowly beginning to heal. Lord Commander Mormont rewards Jon with the Mormont's ancestral sword, Longclaw, a bastard sword made from Valyrian steel. Mormont tells Jon that Barristan has been declared a traitor and has since left King's Landing. He does not tell Jon about his brother Robb's army, but Jon already knows that from Sam, who is in charge of reading Maester Aemon's letters.

Later, Jon is summoned by Maester Aemon. The blind Maester tells him that all men eventually come to a difficult decision: to choose between love, or honor. He tells Jon that he himself had to make that choice, a long time ago. Jon listens to the Maester's tales, and soon come to the startling realization: Master Aemon is a Targaryen.

## Chapter 61- Daenerys

Daenerys rides into Lhazareen, a town recently conquered by Drogo.
Daenerys saves the women from being raped by the Dothraki
warriors. She then finds Drogo with his riders. Drogo has suffered a
cut on his chest. When asked where the healers are, Drogo tells her
that he sent them away, to heal other warriors first. She begs him to
find a healer to sew up his wound. A woman that she has earlier
saved, by the name of Mirri Maz Duur, volunteers to clean up and
sew Drogo's wound. Initially she is met with contempt by Drogo's
bloodriders, who spit on the ground and call her a witch, but
Daenerys manages to convince Drogo to let Mirri tend to his wound.

## Chapter 62 – Tyrion

Tyrion and his clansmen are to take on the vanguard of the attack
against the Stark army. He meets his new squire, a shy boy by the
name of Prodick Payne. Bronn also introduces him to Shae – Tyrion
had earlier told Bronn to help find him a prostitute. Tyrion is
delighted with Shae's wit and beauty.

Tyrion is rudely awaked the next morning by the loud blare of war
horns. He dons his armor and leads the clansmen into battle. The
Lannisters win the battle, and Tyrion is somewhat surprised that he
has managed to survive. When reports come in, it is learned that
Robb was never in this battle; the majority of the Stark army were
now on the other side of the Green Fork, riding to Riverrun.

# Chapter 63 – Catelyn

Robb goes over the battle plans with his bannermen. They report that Jaime Lannister has split his army into three to lay siege to Riverrun. They suggest laying a trap for Jaime Lannister; his bannermen agree that it is a trap the Kingslayer would definitely fall for because Jaime has a reputation for riding out with his scouts, never content to just stay at camp. And true enough, the trap works and they capture Jaime Lannister. Theon suggests killing Jaime. Robb disagrees, stating that Jaime will be more use to them alive than dead.

# Chapter 64 – Daenerys

Drogo does not follow Mirri Maz Duur's instructions on the care of his wound. He becomes delirious with pain, even dropping off from his horse, a bad omen for born riders like the Dothraki. Daenerys orders her bodyguards to take Drogo to a covered tent, away from the eyes of others. She then orders them to bring Mirri Maz Duur to the tent. Jorah enters and removes the poultice from Drogo's chest, only to discover that the chest wound is festering. He warns Daenerys that Drogo will be dead very soon. He also tells her that the best thing to do now would be for both of them to leave the khalasar; if Drogo dies, the other Khals will kill her once they take control of the khalasar. When Daenerys asks why, Jorah tells her that the other Khals will want no competition from her baby.

Mirri arrives but states that there is nothing she can do for Drogo. Daenerys begs her to save him. Mirri proposes a bloodmagic ritual, but warns Daenerys that the price is steep, for it involves death. Daenerys agrees, ignorant of the true price. Mirri instructs everyone to leave the tent and forbids them from entering. Ghostly shadows and screams can be heard in the tent. Drogo's bloodriders try to enter the tent, intending to kill Mirri, but Daenerys and her bloodriders stop them – some of them die in the process. Daenerys goes into labor, but none of the birthing women dare come. Bereft of choices, Jorah carries Daenerys into the Khal's tent despite Mirri's warning.

# Chapter 65 – Arya

Arya has been hiding in King's Landing all this while, surviving by catching and eating pigeons. One day, she sees a crowd of people rushing to the Great Sept of Baelor, and so she follows too. She sees King Joffrey, the Queen and Sansa. They are flanked by the Kingsguard and Lord Petyr and Varys. Eddard is brought out to face the crowd. He confesses to his crimes and proclaims Joffrey the true king.

Joffrey then tells the crowd that his bride, Sansa, has requested mercy for her father. The Queen, he tells them, has requested that Eddard be allowed to join the Night's Watch. Joffrey, however, goes against both of their wishes, and orders Ilyn Payne to execute Eddard. Sansa faints, Varys and the Queen protest, and Arya finds herself roughly manhandled into an alley by Yoren.

# Chapter 66 – Bran

Bran tells Maester Luwin about his dreams; he has been having dreams of walking down into the Stark family crypt and seeing his father there. Maester Luwin then brings Bran, carried by Osha, down into the family crypt, to prove him wrong. As they walk in the crypt, Maester Luwin is suddenly attacked by Shaggydog; Rickon and his direwolf have been staying in the crypt as. When asked the reason for doing so, Rickon mentions that it is because he saw their father, Eddard, in the crypt. Maester Luwin convinces everyone to go back up. A raven brings bad news: Eddard had been executed.

# Chapter 67 – Sansa

Sansa has been staying in her room for days, weeping and grieving. Joffrey summons her and brings her to the battlements, where he forces her to look at her father's head sitting atop an iron spike. Joffrey then tells her he will bring her the head of her brother, Robb Stark, as a gift. Sansa snaps and says that perhaps Robb will give her Joffrey's head instead. Joffrey orders one of the Kingsguard to slap her for her insolence. Sansa notices that Joffrey is at the edge of the battlements; she attempts to push him off, but her attempt fails when the Hounds steps in between the both of them, offering her a tissue to wipe the blood on her lips.

# Chapter 68 – Daenerys

Daenerys wakes up from a long, deep sleep. She asks to see her son, but Ser Jorah tells her that her son is dead. When pressed for further details, Jorah cannot answer, but Mirri Maz Duur does. She tells Daenerys that the child was born deformed, with wings, and the skin fell off from the bones: this was the true price for Drogo's life. Daenerys demands that Mirri brings her to see Drogo. When they go outside, they see that the khalasar is no more; the few that remain are mostly the old and infirm.

They find Drogo outside, staring at the sun. Daenerys is horrified when she realizes that Drogo is now blind. Furious, she orders Mirri to be bound and carried back to camp. When night comes, she uses every trick that she can think of to breathe life back into Drogo. But he never even acknowledges her presence. With tears in her eyes, she smothers him with a cushion.

# Chapter 69 – Tyrion

Tywin has been rapidly marching south, trying to bolster Jamie's forces. He soon hears new of Jamie's capture as well as the breaking of the Riverrun siege. Tywin's bannermen offer many suggestion but he orders them to leave the war council, save for Tyrion and Tywin's brother, Kevan. Tywin reveals that Renly Baratheon has left King's Landing – he has married Margaery Tyrell and proclaimed himself King, with the full power of the Tyrells behind him. He also reveals unsettling rumors that Stannis is gathering a force at Dragonstone. Tywin decides to deal with Robb's army first. He orders Tyrion to go to King's Landing, to rule in his stead, but warns Tyrion not to bring Shae to the King's court. Tyrion decides to go against his father's orders in regards to Shae.

# Chapter 70 – Jon

Jon decides to sneak off in the night, to join up with Robb's army. Sam and the rest of Jon's friends stop him, however. They shame him by repeating the vows he made when he was raised to the Night's Watch, vows that pledge loyalty and service. Jon Snow gives up and returns to Castle Black.

In the morning, Jeor Mormont tells Jon that he is not surprised by Jon's actions; in fact, he had been expecting it. He had also expected Jon to be back by morning. Jeor then tells Jon that a lot of strange things have been happening North of the Wall, and that he intends to lead a large expedition beyond the Wall, to find the truth behind Benjen's disappearance. Jon, ashamed of his actions, agrees to join the expedition, and promises the Commander that he will never run away again.

# Chapter 71 - Catelyn

Catelyn is in Riverrun. She pays a visit to the ruler of Riverrun, her father, Lord Hoster Tully. Her father is happy to see her but sad that Lysa is not with her. After praying in the godswood to mourn of the death of his father, Robb Stark convenes a war council, with all the great lords of the North and the Riverlands in attendance. They discuss their next plan of action. No one can agree to one plan. Robb does not want to support Renly, because by right, Stannis has the true claim. The Greatjon then states that Robb Stark is the only King he'd follow. The great lords all agree and fall to their knees, swearing fealty to Robb Stark and proclaiming him as King of the North.

# Chapter 72 – Daenerys

Daenerys prepares a pyre for Drogo. A horse is killed and placed on top of the pyre. Her three dragon eggs have been laid around Drogo's body. Jorah pleads with Daenerys not to sacrifice herself but she gently tells him that is not her intent. She then calls for Mirri Maz Duur to be placed on the pyre, as well. A red comet flashes over the sky. Daenerys then sets the pyre on fire. The fire starts to grow into a fierce inferno and Mirri Maz Duur screams as she is burned alive. Daenerys walks into the inferno.

Later, once the fire has turned everything to ashes, Daenerys reappears; her hair and clothes have burnt away, but she is otherwise very much alive. And there is something else. She has 3 baby dragons on her body, two suckling her breasts and the other wrapped itself around her shoulder. Seeing the wondrous sight before them, Ser Jorah and the few remaining Dothraki immediately fall to their knees, swearing fealty to Daenerys.

# About BookCaps

We all need refreshers every now and then. Whether you are a student trying to cram for that big final, or someone just trying to understand a book more, BookCaps can help. We are a leader in electronic study guides. Visit www.bookcaps.com to see more of our books, or contact us with any questions.

Made in the USA
Lexington, KY
14 December 2012